SIGN TO LEARN

SIGN TO LEARN

AMERICAN SIGN LANGUAGE IN THE EARLY CHILDHOOD CLASSROOM

KIRSTEN DENNIS & TRESSA AZPIRI

Redleaf Press®
www.redleafpress.org
800-423-8309

Published by Redleaf Press
10 Yorkton Court
St. Paul, MN 55117
www.redleafpress.org

First edition published 2005
Illustrations by Becky Radtke
Cover photo by Steve Wewerka
Cover design by Percolator
Interior design and typesetting by Percolator
The interior of this book was typeset in Whitman and Gotham.
Printed in the United States of America
18 17 16 15 14 13 12 11   5 6 7 8 9 10 11 12

Library of Congress Cataloging-in-Publication Data

Dennis, Kirsten.
    Sign to learn : American Sign Language in the early childhood classroom / Kirsten Dennis, Tressa Azpiri.
       p. cm.
    Includes bibliographical references and index.
    ISBN 978-1-929610-69-3 (pbk.)
    1. American Sign Language. 2. American Sign Language—Study and teaching (Early childhood).
    3. Early childhood education.   I. Azpiri, Tressa. II. Title.
    HV2474.D46 2005
    372.6—dc22   2005006094

Printed on acid-free paper

CONTENTS

Foreword. vii

Acknowledgments. ix

Introduction. 1

Sign Language Terms 4

Chapter 1: History of American Sign Language 5

What Is Deafness?. 5

How Did American Sign Language Develop?. 6

Why Was American Sign Language Controversial? 6

How Was American Sign Language Finally Accepted?. 7

How Did This Change Deaf Education? 7

Chapter 2: Research on Teaching Sign Language to Hearing Children. 9

Deaf and Hearing Students Together 9

Children with Special Needs 10

Second-Language Learners 10

Babies and Toddlers. 10

Early Literacy 11

Chapter 3: Guiding Principles of the American Sign Language Curriculum. 13

Start Early. 13

Start Simple 14

Make It Fun 14

Make It Meaningful. 14

Include Information about People Who Are Deaf 15

Use American Sign Language 15

Use Existing Classroom Materials. 15

Include All Teachers and Staff Members 16

Share with Families. 16

Relax!. 16

Signs for "It's Raining, It's Pouring" 17

Chapter 4: Teaching and Learning about American Sign Language and Deaf Culture 19

Why Teach about Deafness and Deaf Culture?. 19

Learning about Deaf Culture 20

Teaching about Deaf Culture. 22

Learning American Sign Language. 23

Lesson Plan—"Sign Time" 27

Chapter 5: American Sign Language in an Early Childhood Literacy Program 29

Why It Works 29

How to Include ASL in an Early Childhood Literacy Program 30

Literacy Signs 33

Chapter 6: American Sign Language for Classroom Management 37

Engage Your Students 37

Effectively Redirect Behavior 38

Establish Routines 38

Ease Transitions 38

Address Different Learning Styles 39

Increase Communication with Children with Special Needs 39

Create a Common Language in a Multilingual Classroom 40

Help Children Understand and Express Feelings 40

Calm the Classroom 40

Build Community 41

Classroom Management Signs 41

Chapter 7: Thematic Lesson Plans 49

The ASL Illustrations 49

Unit Order 50

Introducing ASL Vocabulary 50

Using Children's Books 50

Songs 50

A Final Word 51

Feelings 53

Family 65

School 87

Food 103

Colors 119

Seasons 133

Community Helpers 159

Animals 175

Appendix I: American Sign Language Illustration Index 188

Appendix II: Sample Letter to Families 191

Appendix III: References 192

Appendix IV: Resources 193

FOREWORD

It is a pleasure for me to see *Sign to Learn* make its debut. It is my hope and belief that it will greatly benefit early childhood teachers. I have worked directly with Kirsten Dennis and Tressa Azpiri to share Deaf culture with their early childhood students. I have been pleased and impressed with their respectful approach of using American Sign Language (ASL) in all aspects of their program and in their seeking direct input from Deaf individuals about the appropriateness of the curriculum.

Sign to Learn will enable other hearing teachers without a sign language background to begin implementing the beautiful and visual language of ASL and to begin understanding Deaf culture with a fresh, innovative perspective. In this book, Kirsten Dennis and Tressa Azpiri provide research findings that show how ASL helps students with early literacy skills. They describe the value of exposing young hearing children to another culture and language. In addition, they explain how the implementation of ASL in the hearing classroom has proved to have a great impact on changing the tone of the classroom, which I'm sure many teachers will be thrilled to discover! Signing in an early childhood classroom allows children to focus within a quieter, calmer environment.

This thoughtfully written and simple approach for including sign language in an early childhood program will be of immense benefit to both students and teachers. It describes innovative ways for early childhood educators to include signing in their educational activities and classroom management strategies. Every early childhood teacher who seeks a calmer teaching and learning environment, more effective methods for teaching academic skills to young children, and a fun introduction to a different language and culture should have a copy of this curriculum in her classroom.

Enjoy!

Billy Seago
Director, Deaf Youth Drama Program
Seattle Children's Theatre

ACKNOWLEDGMENTS

This book began as Kirsten's master's thesis, documenting Tressa's innovative sign language program for young hearing children. Professor Fran Davidson and Dr. John Nimmo, formerly of Pacific Oaks College Northwest, guided the direction of this work. Thank you to all the children of Puddle Stompers School on Vashon Island, Washington. It was the joy of sharing ASL with you in a loving and peaceful environment that first inspired the writing of this book. Many thanks to Billy and Liza Seago for sharing their language and culture with us and our students. Thanks also to Beth Wallace and Redleaf Press for thinking this book was a good idea and helping us share our work with other early childhood educators. Finally, we appreciate our families, especially our "Abby and Jazzy girls," for their patience and support.

INTRODUCTION

At nine o'clock on a warm spring morning, several young children enter their classroom, cheerfully greeting one another and their teachers. They put their belongings away in small cubbies near the door and settle into a playtime activity. A few children work on puzzles, some hold the classroom animals, and others read books in a cozy corner. There is a peaceful hum of talking and playing. After several minutes, the lead teacher goes to the light switch and flicks the lights off and on a few times. The children stop their activities and look up at her. She instructs them to clean up and come to the story time rug without using her voice at all.

This is American Sign Language in an early childhood classroom.

A teacher sits with a group of four-year-old children. They sing an ABC song and make the letter shapes with their fingers. The teacher holds up cards with words and pictures on them. Slowly the children say the letters together and make the letter shape with their hands as they pronounce the sounds. They read and sign the word.

This is American Sign Language in an early childhood classroom.

Two young children are playing together with blocks. They are busy making roads, tall buildings, and a large fire station. Another child comes over and knocks down one of their buildings. One of the children who was building stands up, stomps his feet, makes an angry face, and raises his shaking hands up to his head. He is furious, and he has just communicated that without screaming or hitting.

This is American Sign Language in an early childhood classroom.

If you are reading this book, you may have already heard stories like these and more about how teachers are incorporating sign language into their early childhood programs. You may have noticed parents or caregivers signing to hearing babies and toddlers and watched with curiosity this unique way of communicating. Perhaps you have shared with the children in your program books or videos that included sign language and noticed their interest in mimicking the movements. Or maybe you have deaf or hearing impaired students or family members in your program and you want to learn more about communicating with sign language and creating an inclusive classroom. Regardless of the reason, if you are ready to begin the journey of teaching and learning sign language with young children, this book will show you the way.

Sign languages use facial expressions and hand and body movements to communicate feelings, thoughts, and ideas. There are different forms of sign language that can be used with young hearing children. Some educators teach what is known as Signed Exact English, or SEE. SEE was created by hearing people and uses signing gestures for words but keeps English word order in sentences. Hearing teachers may feel that SEE is easier for them to learn and that it is more appropriate for young children to learn a second language that follows a "hearing" sentence structure. Teachers may use SEE with hearing children while speaking at the same time, and the children can see how the hand gestures relate to the spoken words.

However, we strongly advocate the use of American Sign Language (ASL) in early childhood classrooms. American Sign Language is the preferred form of communication for people who are deaf in the United States. ASL was created by deaf people and is a unique and beautiful language that uses hand shapes, motion, and facial expressions to communicate *visual* concepts. In addition, like other languages, ASL is deeply rooted in Deaf community and culture. (A capital "D" is typically used when writing "Deaf" in the context of a community or a culture. A lowercase "d" is used for "deaf," to indicate the physical condition.) As we will explain in the first chapter, American Sign Language has a complex and controversial history. For many years ASL was not viewed as a real language and its use was banned in Deaf education. Deaf people have suffered from that fact and have struggled to have ASL accepted as a true language. Because of this, many people who are deaf feel their identity is deeply connected to their use of American Sign Language. For hearing educators using ASL with hearing students, it is important to understand and respect Deaf language, history, and culture. The information and activities presented in this book will help you and your students achieve this understanding.

American Sign Language has a place in early childhood classrooms with hearing children for many reasons. First of all, by using correct ASL and teaching children about deafness and Deaf culture, we can help children accept and appreciate differences between people. If your program includes children, family, or staff members who are deaf or hearing impaired, or if all the students are hearing, teaching and learning ASL shows respect for diversity, promotes interactions between deaf and hearing people, and stretches children's awareness and empathy.

Secondly, early childhood is an ideal time to begin sign language instruction. Young children are ready for language learning. When children use sign language while learning letters of the alphabet and words, this early literacy learning is enhanced. And sign language is active! Child development specialist Jean Piaget tells us that movement is the true language of childhood. Signing addresses young children's need to use their bodies while learning. Furthermore, as early childhood teachers we know that children learn in different ways. ASL allows a teacher to present information visually and through hand and body movements and gives children additional ways to understand what they are being taught. Children benefit from being able to process information with all of their senses.

In addition, including sign language in an early childhood curriculum can be a valuable classroom management tool. Using hand movements with young children helps grab their attention and encourages them to focus on the teacher. Signing quiets down the noise level in the classroom and can allow teachers to redirect unwanted behavior without disrupting the rest of the class. Sign language can also give children a new way to express their thoughts and feelings.

These facts may explain why sign language is so interesting to young children. Teachers integrating ASL into their early childhood programs are amazed to see how the language seems so natural and understandable for the children. Children are very enthusiastic about learning sign language and often proudly share their new skills with their families at home. This creates a wonderful opportunity for teachers to make connections between school and home.

All of this sounds fantastic, and you probably cannot wait to get started. But where do you begin? The problem for many early childhood teachers who may understand why their students would benefit from learning sign language is how to develop and implement a sign language curriculum for young hearing children. How much ASL do you need to know to begin? How do you address deafness and Deaf cultural sensitivity with hearing children? How do you integrate signing into academic lessons and play activities? How do you use sign language for classroom management? Do you need to purchase sign language materials and resources? How can learning American Sign Language help your students with special needs? In this curriculum guide we have answered these questions and more.

Together we have over twenty years' experience sharing sign language with young children. We have both taught preschool and kindergarten classes in public and private settings and worked with hundreds of children and families. We have successfully incorporated sign language into our programs with typically developing hearing children from three to six years old. In addition, we have included signing in our work with students with special needs, including hearing impairments, delayed speech, mild mental retardation, autism, and children who are learning English as a second language.

We started using sign language with our students when we knew only a few signs. We learned the language (and are still learning) right along with our students. It began with using sign language hand signals for classroom management directions such as *sit down, line up, quiet voice, time for lunch,* and the all-important *stop it now!* As we used these signs and as the children understood them, we found that we appreciated not having to raise our voices to communicate with a child across the room. Also, being able to quietly redirect behavior and give directions created a calmer classroom environment.

We then began to find different ways to include sign language in our daily activities in the classroom. We learned signs for words to our weekly chart poems, songs, and repetitive vocabulary in story books. We taught sign language vocabulary with flashcards and real objects. We noticed that whenever we did sign language activities the children were very attentive, focused, engaged, and quiet for the duration of the activity. We were hooked!

We are both hearing women, and although we have been learning ASL for many years, we are still not fluent. However, by using good ASL dictionaries, taking classes, and learning from friends who are deaf, we have managed to acquire enough signing skills to design and implement a successful curriculum program. Our work with some children and family members who are deaf has given us important insight to the issues involved in creating a curriculum that is culturally sensitive. From them we have learned more about using ASL correctly and respectfully and why doing so is important.

We now integrate American Sign Language learning into most of the daily activities in our classrooms, including our early literacy program, math, art, plays, songs, games, snack time, calendar—even "Show and Tell"! The children in our classrooms have the opportunity to learn a new language, understand a different culture, express themselves in a unique way, and learn with all of their senses.

Teaching and learning American Sign Language with young deaf and hearing children has been an exciting adventure for us, and we continue to learn more each school year, with every new group of children. Because of the overwhelm-

ingly positive impact learning and sharing ASL has had on our personal and professional lives, and the lives of the students and families we work with, we felt it would be worthwhile to share our curriculum with others.

Together we spent an entire year documenting in depth our American Sign Language curriculum for early childhood education. We examined the philosophy behind the instruction, our methods for developing lesson plans, how we make learning sign language fun and meaningful for young hearing children, and how we teach children about deafness and Deaf culture. We identified the benefits of including sign language in academic activities and classroom management. And finally we recorded and organized all the sign language lesson plans we have used over the years.

So let's begin! The first two chapters will provide you with some important background to help you further understand why sharing American Sign Language with your students is valuable and rewarding. Chapter 1 includes a brief history of the development of American Sign Language, its controversial use in Deaf education, and its importance in Deaf community and culture. It is an emotional and interesting story that we encourage you to examine before you begin any kind of sign language curriculum with hearing students. Chapter 2 details research that shows how hearing children benefit from learning sign language and includes information about signing for children with special needs, babies, and toddlers, and how signing enhances early literacy skills.

In chapters 3, 4, 5, and 6 we present our American Sign Language curriculum for the early childhood classroom. Chapter 3 details the guiding principles of the curriculum and includes additional information about the benefits of using ASL in an early childhood program, as well as specific examples from our own classrooms. Chapter 4 offers information about teaching hearing children about deafness and Deaf culture, and many tips for teachers learning ASL. In chapter 5 we provide details about how to include signing into an early childhood literacy program. Ideas on how to use sign language for classroom management are discussed in chapter 6, along with details of the many advantages of using these methods.

Chapter 7 includes a school year's worth of sign language lesson plans, arranged thematically, with detailed instructions for teaching the lessons, material lists, follow-up activities, and illustrations for how to do the signs (see page 49 for tips on using the ASL illustrations in this book, and page 188 for a complete sign illustration index). The activities are intended to be used in an early childhood classroom with children aged three to six. Also included in this curriculum guide is a comprehensive sign language resource list, with a list of useful children's books, sign language dictionaries, ASL curriculum materials, and recommendations for further reading.

We hope you will be inspired by this book and come to understand that teaching and learning American Sign Language with young hearing children is easy and fun! You do not need to be fluent in the language or invest a lot of money in new materials to be successful. With this curriculum guide and a good ASL dictionary, you can start sharing this wonderful language with the children in your program right away.

SIGN LANGUAGE TERMS

You may have already noticed there are several terms we use when writing about sign language, and that the words can appear in different forms, some with capital letters and some not. Here is a short glossary to help explain these terms:

sign language—With no capital letters, refers to the broad category of languages that are not spoken. Like the term "foreign language" it does not refer to any specific language. For example, "They were communicating with sign language."

American Sign Language (ASL)—The sign language used by the Deaf community in the United States. This term is always capitalized, as it refers to a specific name of a language, like "English" or "Spanish."

Signed Exact English (SEE)—A way of using signs to convey the English language. SEE is not a language itself.

Sign—With a capital "S" refers to the name of a language, but it could be American Sign Language or Signed Exact English or another form of signing. It is capitalized to distinguish it from lowercase "sign" (see below) which refers to a specific movement made to communicate an idea.

sign/signing—(verb) No capitals because each is used as a verb the same way you would write "talk" or "speaking."

sign/signs—(noun) These refer to the specific movements made to communicate a word. English has "words." American Sign Language has "signs."

CHAPTER 1

HISTORY

OF AMERICAN SIGN LANGUAGE

American Sign Language (ASL) is the most commonly used language for people who are deaf in the United States. For many deaf people, the shared use of ASL binds them together as a community and helps define what is known as "Deaf culture." When hearing teachers consider using ASL with their hearing or deaf students, they need to be aware of the history of the language and the importance of ASL in Deaf culture. In addition, teachers should know about a view of deafness that does not define being deaf as having a disease or a defect, but instead values deafness as a shared cultural characteristic. The background information presented in this chapter is important. We know you will find it compelling and hope that you will keep this perspective in mind when you include ASL in your teaching.

WHAT IS DEAFNESS?

Deafness can be defined as the inability to hear sound. There are varying degrees of deafness, ranging from mild hearing loss to severe hearing loss. People can lose their sense of hearing through illness, trauma, infection, or aging. Hearing loss present at birth sometimes happens because of prenatal infection or heredity. Deafness has been traditionally described as a medical defect, and people who are deaf are often viewed as disabled. This view of deafness as disease or deficiency has created several negative consequences for people who are deaf.

You have probably heard the phrase "deaf and dumb," referring to the fact that most deaf people could not speak. Because they could not speak, people who were deaf were considered to have no language at all and therefore no ability to think. History shows that this view of deafness continued for hundreds of years, with few exceptions. Laws existed that forbade people who were deaf from marrying or owning property. No attempt was made to educate deaf people, and many lived isolated and poor lives.

Today, some psychologists still describe deafness as a form of mental retardation, and scientists are hard at work developing new hearing devices and artificial eardrums in order to "cure" being deaf. In addition, many children who are born deaf have hearing parents. Viewing deafness as a disease can cause hearing parents to want to "fix" their child's deafness by forcing speech and lipreading or providing hearing aids and cochlear implants.

For many people who are deaf, deafness is not an illness, or a problem; rather, being Deaf (with a capital D) defines their identity and culture. Sign languages are considered critical to Deaf identity and a unifying and necessary element of their cultural group. All around the world, sign languages have been created and used by deaf people to communicate thoughts, feelings, and ideas. Through signing, people who are deaf tell stories, express emotion, record history, share humor, and construct a common bond of language that makes them part of a community.

HOW DID AMERICAN SIGN LANGUAGE DEVELOP?

The history of American Sign Language actually begins in France, around 1770, with a priest named Abbé Charles Michel de L'Epée. Ministering to poor people in Paris, he met two girls who were deaf and could not speak. De L'Epée became interested in trying to communicate with them. He first learned the signs they were already producing, and then invented signs to add to their vocabulary using French grammar. With this method he was able to teach the girls and his future students to read and write French.

De L'Epée established a school in Paris and based his educational methods on the belief that signing had to be the language of the deaf people. He knew sign language was invented by them and thought that only through signing could deaf people learn to read, write, and communicate. In addition, De L'Epée was one of the first people to question the intelligence of deaf people and suggest they were not inherently "dumb" but simply lacked an understandable way to communicate.

During this same period of history (late 1700s to early 1800s), wealthy deaf people in America would go to England to be schooled in the "oral methods" tradition. These methods were based on the desire to teach deaf people to speak and speech read. Instructors used little or no sign language.

As De L'Epée's methods for educating deaf students became more popular and accepted in Europe, Thomas Hopkins Gallaudet, a minister from New England interested in the education of deaf people, traveled to France and met a young, intelligent, and articulate deaf man named Laurent Clerc. Clerc agreed to come back to America

with Gallaudet and teach him the French method of signing. They established, in 1817, the American Asylum in Hartford, Connecticut, and Clerc became the first deaf teacher of deaf students in America. Together, Clerc and Gallaudet created a new sign language, mixing the French signs with the signs used by Deaf Americans of the time. They called it American Sign Language.

Laurent Clerc is, to this day, a cultural hero of the Deaf community. He is considered a founding father in Deaf history—the first to recognize their potential to become educated, literate members of society. Clerc continued to educate deaf children and train (mostly deaf) teachers with the evolving language of American Sign. Many residential Deaf schools and communities were created in the United States, and with them came for the first time the beginning of a shared identity, knowledge, and beliefs—the emergence of a Deaf culture.

WHY WAS AMERICAN SIGN LANGUAGE CONTROVERSIAL?

By 1860, there were about twenty schools for deaf students in America. Public schools based education instruction on the new American Sign Language, but some private deaf schools favored teaching the use of speech and speech reading. So-called oralist schools could be harsh, and students were forbidden from using any form of sign language. Teachers would even slap or tie children's hands or force them to sit on them. However cruel they may have seemed, these methods sometimes produced students who could function well in the hearing world, and controversy erupted over the best way to educate deaf people.

Oralists argued that teaching sign language would allow deaf people to communicate only with each other, making them a separate society. They felt that deaf people would never be motivated to learn speech, since signing was easier for them. In addition, during this time in American history, many immigrants were coming to America from diverse cultures. There was a general opposition to foreign languages and a movement to standardize the English language. American Sign Language was viewed as primitive and immature.

Alexander Graham Bell, known best for inventing the telephone, was a leader of the Oralist movement. The son of a deaf mother, and married to a woman who was deaf, Bell believed deafness to be a tragedy and was concerned with "normalizing" the deaf. Bell believed that technology and scientific advances could "cure" deafness and that deaf people should be integrated into the hearing society by learning to read, write, and speak the English language. In 1880, with the support of Bell and others at an international conference for educators of deaf students, sign language was officially denounced.

Sign language instruction and use were no longer allowed in public schools, and only hearing teachers were permitted to teach deaf students. Students spent long hours on tedious speech and lipreading lessons and they were never allowed to use sign language. The prohibition of sign language in deaf education created an obvious decline in the educational achievement of deaf people. These "Dark Ages," as members of the Deaf community call it, continued for the next eighty years.

HOW WAS AMERICAN SIGN LANGUAGE FINALLY ACCEPTED?

In 1955 William Stokoe arrived at Gallaudet College, America's only higher-education school for deaf people. He came to teach English literature, and ended up saving American Sign Language. At the time of Stokoe's arrival, sign language instruction was still not recommended in deaf education. The president, board members, and faculty at Gallaudet College were mostly hearing people with little knowledge of ASL. However, some professors used a combination of Signed English and speaking when teaching their courses. Stokoe enrolled in a course to learn the basics of Signed English, which is a sign-for-word translation of English.

Stokoe soon noticed, however, that the sign language the students used among themselves was quite different from what he was being taught. When he asked the other teachers about this, he was told to ignore the "primitive gestures" of the students. However, Stokoe believed that he would not be able to teach his students to read and write

English well unless he learned their language. He began reading about sign language history and learning ASL from native signers (people born deaf and exposed to signing from a young age).

In 1960, Stokoe published a study titled "Sign Language Structure," which contained an analysis of American Sign Language and concluded that ASL was a true language. Stokoe found that just like in other languages, which contain "parts of speech" that are used to communicate, American Sign Language has "parts of signs" that can be combined in a variety of ways. Stokoe also published the first dictionary of American Sign Language, which included a description of the cultural and social characteristics of deaf people who used American Sign Language.

HOW DID THIS CHANGE DEAF EDUCATION?

New scientific research demonstrating ASL to be a "real" language, in addition to a social climate during the 1960s and '70s that emphasized equal rights of minority populations, allowed deaf people to begin demanding their right to be recognized as a cultural minority. For teachers of deaf students, this created at least two problems. First, it meant the end of teaching only speech and lipreading and a move toward accepting sign language as an important part of instruction. However, when schools allowed signing back into the classroom, it was not in the form of American Sign Language, but rather, a signed form of English. As we have mentioned before, Signed English uses signs but keeps them in English word order. This type of signing was created by and is mostly used by hearing people and is not considered a true language. For some people in the Deaf community the continued denial of ASL represents the denial of their culture.

Second, the Individuals with Disabilities Education Act led to new laws requiring deaf students to be placed into "regular" education classes. This often meant an end to all-Deaf schools, and a move toward integration with hearing schools. The issue of placing deaf children into hearing schools remains controversial in the Deaf community today. Some argue that Deaf schools provide benefits to deaf children because they function like community centers where Deaf language, cultural beliefs, and values can be shared. Few teachers in hearing schools are fluent in ASL, and many times deaf children are lumped together with other children with "disabilities" and presented a standard special-education curriculum. The result can leave deaf children feeling isolated and alone, cut off from their language and cultural identity.

Despite ongoing controversy, the reality is that most deaf children today do not attend schools for deaf students only. Deaf and hearing children are attending school together, and sign language has found its way into many school programs. As hearing teachers began to use sign language to communicate with the deaf students in their classes, they discovered that signing could benefit their hearing students as well. Now teachers are including sign language in special-education and regular-education classrooms with hearing children of all ages. In the next chapter we will discuss specific ways that some hearing teachers have integrated signing into their instruction and how researchers have found that including sign language in educational programs can benefit all young children in many ways.

RESEARCH

ON TEACHING SIGN LANGUAGE TO HEARING CHILDREN

In chapter 1 you read about the history of American Sign Language, its importance in Deaf culture, and its controversial use in the education of children who are deaf. Today, deaf and hard-of-hearing children are placed into "regular" education classes. Many teachers have discovered that the use of sign language in a classroom setting can lead to benefits not only for children who are deaf but also for hearing children. The goal of this chapter is to tell you about the research that has been done over the past several years, documenting the use of sign language with hearing children.

The first section includes examples of programs that have successfully educated deaf and hearing students together. The next section tells about research showing how sign language can benefit children with special needs. Then we look at research about using sign language with hearing babies and toddlers. Finally, we include examples from the extensive research that has been done about using sign language with hearing children to enhance early literacy skills.

DEAF AND HEARING STUDENTS TOGETHER

At an elementary school in Alaska, during the early

1990s, children in first through sixth grade were involved in a program called "Multigraded Education for Deaf and Hearing Students" (Daniels, 2001). The program included deaf and hearing students learning together in a multiage classroom. The teachers were all hearing but experienced in ASL. Members of the local Deaf community helped the teachers and volunteered to work in the classrooms with the students. The teachers used ASL and English, although ASL became the primary language in the classrooms. All of the students learned to communicate through signing. The teachers and students involved in this program described many benefits of hearing and deaf children learning together in the same class. They found that all the children successfully learned English and ASL. The students who were deaf gained more friends who could communicate with them. Also, the hearing children gained respect and appreciation for ASL and learned about Deaf culture (Daniels, 2001).

Another school program that included deaf and hearing students in the same classroom is described in the article "Let's All Sign: Enhancing Language Development in an Inclusive Preschool" (Heller, Manning, Pavur, and Wagner, 1998). Teachers at Newcomb College Nursery School at Tulane University in New Orleans learned one year that they would have two children who were deaf in their class. They decided they would take the opportunity to learn sign language and teach it to the entire preschool class. The teachers learned Signed English and spoke English while signing during classroom activities and conversation. They also discovered numerous benefits of using sign language with hearing and deaf children. They found that the preschool children in their program increased their vocabulary and understanding of words and letters. In addition, the teachers felt that learning to communicate with sign language improved the social interactions between all the children.

CHILDREN WITH SPECIAL NEEDS

Research shows that using sign language in educational settings is effective with children who have special needs such as delayed speech, autism, Down syndrome, or other learning disabilities. Many educators have discovered that using sign language with hearing children with special needs can improve their communication, academic skills, and social interaction.

At a special-needs preschool in Virginia, teachers used sign language to communicate with children who had severe language delays associated with autism. The teachers used signs as they spoke to give the children directions and teach them new words. Their goal was to use the visual and physical signs for words to help these children understand speech and begin to talk more themselves (Lohmann, 1999).

Special-education teacher Laura Felzer used sign language to teach reading to her students, most of whom were diagnosed with Down syndrome. She had used signs with some of her students who had speech disabilities, and the other students in her class showed great interest in learning the signs as well. Felzer found that if she taught the children the signs for new vocabulary words they were learning to read, they were more likely to remember the words (Felzer, 1998).

SECOND-LANGUAGE LEARNERS

Sign language instruction can help children who do not speak English as their first language. Not only does using signs help children acquire English more easily, it also serves as a bridge between children who are learning English and children whose first language is English, reducing the isolation and segregation of English-language learners.

At a preschool in Buffalo, New York, where 30 percent of the children speak English as a second language (ESL), teachers are including sign language as a main method of communication (Donovan, 2000). They find that signing can serve as a common language for everyone and can increase social interaction among the children. In addition, when teachers present visual signs for specific words while speaking, ESL students learn more English vocabulary. This increased ability to communicate with teachers and peers helps second-language learners feel less frustrated at school.

BABIES AND TODDLERS

The idea of teaching typically developing hearing babies and toddlers to use simple sign language gestures to communicate before they can talk has grown in popularity over the last few years. Children as young as six months can be taught to sign words for everyday objects such as "ball" or "dog," express feelings such as "tired" or "happy," or communicate needs such as "eat" or "more" (Garcia, 1999). Parents and caregivers report that learning to sign can dramatically decrease frustration for babies and toddlers. Adults and young children both benefit when babies' needs are met. Signing can help very young children express their desires clearly!

In addition to the advantage of a less frustrated, more communicative baby, research shows that very young hearing children who learn sign language can increase their "brain power." In a research study titled "Impact of Symbolic Gesturing on Early Language Development," Goodwyn, Acredolo, and Brown (2000) examined the cognitive benefits for very young children learning to sign. They found that babies who were taught to use sign language to communicate talked earlier, used more words, and had higher IQ scores when compared with a group of non-signing children.

EARLY LITERACY

Given that using sign language has so many benefits for babies and toddlers, children with special needs, and English-language learners, it's not surprising that sign language also supports the early literacy of typically developing hearing preschoolers. There is a lot of research to support this point; we will highlight the most relevant studies here.

At the Otter Creek School in Vermont, early childhood teachers Stan and Priscilla Baker used sign language with their hearing students. They signed during music times, used sign language during snack, and taught their students the sign language alphabet to teach letter and sound recognition. In an interview with Gail Ellison (1982), they discuss how adding sign language to their preschool program has helped their students learn literacy skills. They believe that signing letter shapes with their hands helps children understand their abstract meaning. Furthermore, the physical movement of signing gets children to focus on learning and remembering information.

Early childhood teacher Debbie Manning-Beagle (1988) agrees in her article "Learning Through Motion: Sign Language for Young Children." She used sign language in her Head Start preschool class and found it beneficial because signing allowed the children to learn letters and words in a visual and physical way. She also points out that children's enthusiasm for signing is great, and as a teaching tool, it allowed her to grab and hold young children's attention. The children were more engaged in literacy activities when sign language was included.

Kindergarten teacher Barbara Cooper uses sign language to enhance her language arts curriculum. She teaches her students signs for new reading vocabulary and how to use the sign language alphabet to spell words. In a recent article from *The Reading Teacher*, Cooper (2002) states that sign language increases the interest of her hearing students in reading activities. She also finds that signing helps children who do not learn to read

well using only their visual sense. Using their bodies to learn helps many children understand and remember letters and words.

In the book *Signing for Reading Success* (1986), researchers Jan Hafer and Robert Wilson describe a study they conducted with first- and second-grade general-education students who were having difficulty remembering new reading vocabulary. The experiment involved teaching some new vocabulary words with the signs as the teacher read the word, and teaching some words with no signing. The researchers tested the students after fourteen weeks on words taught in the traditional method and words taught with sign language instruction. The results of the research showed that students knew significantly more of the reading vocabulary words they learned with signing.

After experiencing success using sign language to teach reading to her special-education students, Laura Felzer went on to develop a reading program she called "A Multi-Sensory Reading Program That Really Works." Felzer teamed up with kindergarten teacher Ruth Nishida to study whether her multisensory reading program would be effective with a class of general-education students. The teachers tested the students in Ruth's class at the beginning of kindergarten and found that none of the twenty-five children could identify any letters of the alphabet, phonetic sounds, or words. Ruth and Laura worked together to implement the reading program, which included using sign language when teaching new vocabulary, simple sentences, and letter names and sounds. When they tested the kindergarteners again in May they found that twenty-one of the twenty-five students were reading at a first-grade level (Felzer, 1998).

In her book, *Dancing with Words: Signing for Hearing Children's Literacy* (2001), Dr. Marilyn Daniels, a professor of communications at Pennsylvania State University, documents ten years of her research on using sign language to teach literacy skills to hearing children. In one of her research studies, "The Effect of Sign Language on Hearing Children's Language Development" (1994), she compared the reading vocabulary of two groups of pre-kindergarten students. One group received sign language instruction during reading activities and one did not. Results from this research showed that the students receiving sign language instruction in their pre-kindergarten curriculum scored significantly higher on vocabulary tests than the students with no signing instruction. Additionally, Daniels has documented other advantages to including signing in literacy activities, such as increased focus and engagement of the students, and the children's ability to learn signs quickly and remember them easily.

As you can see, many teachers and researchers have found that teaching sign language to hearing children has a positive impact on their education. Inclusive programs can successfully teach deaf and hearing children together, allowing greater appreciation for diversity of languages and abilities. Learning sign language increases communication for children with special needs and helps second-language learners with English-speaking skills. Signing enhances typical students' early literacy learning and is an engaging and motivating form of instruction.

Now that you've read through these first chapters of our book, we hope you have been inspired by the history of the special language of ASL, the story of the people who use it, and tales of teachers successfully including ASL in their work with hearing and deaf students. And now that you are aware of the extensive research that shows how teaching and learning sign language can benefit you and your students, let's get started learning how to make it happen!

CHAPTER 3

GUIDING PRINCIPLES

OF THE AMERICAN SIGN LANGUAGE CURRICULUM

We begin this description of our American Sign Language curriculum for young hearing children with ten guiding principles for you to consider. Keep these ideas in your mind while you share ASL with your hearing students or in your deaf/hearing inclusive classroom.

1. Start early.

2. Start simple.

3. Make it fun.

4. Make it meaningful.

5. Include information about people who are deaf.

6. Use American Sign Language.

7. Use existing classroom materials.

8. Include all teachers and staff members.

9. Share with families.

10. Relax!

START EARLY

It is a great idea to start using sign language as early as possible in the school year. This helps model the expectations for the classroom and allows children to see signing as a normal part of the way they communicate at school. Using sign language while you talk engages children to focus on what you are saying. Sign language calms down the classroom environment. Children learn that you do not want or need to raise your voice to be heard. Including sign language while speaking basic classroom management phrases, like "sit down," "walking feet," and "quiet voice," helps children tune in to these directions and sets the stage for simple and silent redirecting of unwanted behavior in the future.

You can begin by simply singing a familiar song, like "It's Raining, It's Pouring" (see p. 17) when you are all gathered together for circle time. Sing and sign the words at the same time. Most children are familiar with the song and will try to follow along with the sign motions. After you sing and sign it a few times say, "Let's lock our voices and sing the song with our hands." Show the children how to put their hands to their throats and make a "click" sound while they pretend to "turn the key" on their voice box. This motion becomes the signal to get ready to use sign language. Then use your hands without your voices to do the song. The children will love it and be on their way to learning a new way to communicate!

START SIMPLE

When you first introduce signing to the young hearing children in your class, it is not necessary to include specific information about the language or people who might use it. Discussion of ASL as the language used by people who are deaf is important and should be included with future lessons, but in the beginning, just do it! The idea is for children to see signing as a natural and fun way to communicate.

At first we use our voice together with signing during most activities. Singing and signing familiar songs and signing a few repetitive words while reading story books are both easy ways to begin introducing sign language vocabulary. Early activities are primarily receptive—meaning the children are watching the teacher make the signs and learning the vocabulary. This does not mean that their little hands should not and will not be very busy mimicking everything you do! It does not take long for young hearing children to master this "language in motion."

As the year progresses and the children develop a larger vocabulary and understanding of sign language, you can begin to include more opportunities for the children to use the signs they have learned. Incorporate more expressive activities, where the children present the signs for you or other children to understand, and more details about the differences between ASL and English.

MAKE IT FUN

Young hearing children are very motivated to learn ASL, and engaging them in signing activities is not difficult. Even so, we do need to be mindful of the developmental needs of the children we work with and provide appropriate experiences. A successful sign language curriculum has the same basic philosophy as any early childhood curriculum: that young children learn best through hands-on, play-based activities. We recommend teaching ASL through the use of games, stories, songs, and everyday classroom routines and experiences.

For example, you can take a common game like Simon Says and turn it into a fun sign language activity (see p. 69). By teaching signs for different body parts (head, arm, hand, foot, leg) and movements (jump, run, step, turn around, skip, sit down) you can play Simon Signs! It is an active participation game that requires no materials but teaches a lot of useful ASL vocabulary, and children really like it.

MAKE IT MEANINGFUL

One of the goals for a successful early childhood sign language program is for children to view signing as a natural part of the way they communicate at school. Signing should not only be taught through isolated activities, but should also be integrated into existing curriculum in meaningful ways. Including sign language during daily activities such as calendar (see p. 133), reading (see p. 35), or "Show and Tell" (see p. 31) makes ASL learning relevant and ongoing. In addition, it is practical to balance teacher-directed large-group sign language activities with opportunities for children to practice their signing skills throughout the day. For example, you can sign ASL vocabulary for colors (see p. 126) while children explore the art center or food signs (see p. 110) during snack.

When deciding on what new ASL vocabulary you would like to introduce, try to teach signs that correspond to your current themes of study. A great activity for introducing new sign language vocabulary based on themes is what we call the "Basket Game" (see p. 31). It involves collecting (in a basket or bin) small objects or pictures that represent the signs you want to teach. For example: pretend food, school supplies, plastic animals, or toy people. The items in the basket can be changed weekly, or monthly, depending on what you are studying, and you can add new items as needed. This game is usually played as a whole group, with the teacher introducing the signs while showing the object or picture and the children making the signs. Children then have a turn to pick out the correct object based on the sign the teacher shows them.

This lesson works well with young hearing children. They learn the signs quickly and remember them easily. Introducing new signs based on themes and reinforcing those signs using books and songs of the same theme help the children make connections and solidify the concepts in their minds. In chapter 7 we have included groups of lesson plans that center on common early childhood themes, such as families, food, seasons, and colors, and include suggestions for corresponding books and songs.

INCLUDE INFORMATION ABOUT PEOPLE WHO ARE DEAF

Because of the connection ASL has to the culture of many people who are deaf, hearing teachers must work to help their hearing students understand deafness and appreciate Deaf culture. Many people who are deaf do not define themselves as disabled but as members of a distinct population, rich with tradition, culture, and language. Including this perspective when using sign language with hearing children or in a deaf/hearing inclusive classroom creates an environment where diversity is valued, differences are accepted, and awareness is deepened.

Our early childhood sign language curriculum provides accurate information about people who are deaf and sensitively explores commonalities and differences between deaf and hearing people. By directly teaching appropriate use of ASL, including members of the Deaf community as advisors or volunteers, and using books and activities that illustrate Deaf cultural norms, we can provide a curriculum that respects Deaf language and culture. The next chapter in this book specifically details these methods and further explains the rationale behind this very important guiding principle.

USE AMERICAN SIGN LANGUAGE

This may sound obvious, but as we mentioned in the introduction, some hearing educators use other forms of sign language, invented by hearing people, that follow English language structure, with their hearing students. ASL is a visual language created by deaf people and used every day by deaf and hearing people to express thoughts, ideas, opinions, and feelings. One of the most meaningful

ways to show respect to Deaf culture as a hearing person using sign language with hearing students is to use true ASL and use it correctly.

Our curriculum emphasizes the accurate use of ASL. Don't worry; we don't mean that you have to be a fluent signer or an expert on Deaf culture to start signing with your students! We just want to give you the tools to create a meaningful program that uses the language of another culture with care and respect. For example, remember not to "make up" signs, use ASL dictionaries instead of Signed English references, and teach lessons that illustrate the differences between ASL (a visual language) and English (a spoken language). You will find all these methods and more details in chapter 4.

USE EXISTING CLASSROOM MATERIALS

It is not necessary for teachers to purchase a lot of new classroom materials in order to implement a successful sign language program for young hearing children. As we mentioned previously, an appropriate ASL curriculum can be based in familiar early childhood play activities, songs, books, and games and integrated into existing daily routines. Our lessons do include the use of children's books about deafness, sign language, and early childhood themes, but these books and more can be obtained through your local library. However, we do strongly recommend the purchase of one or two ASL dictionaries, such as *The Picture Plus Dictionary* (McKinney & Vega, 1997) or the *American Sign Language Dictionary* (Sternberg, 1981).

Many times as we considered new sign language activities, we just took something we were already doing and merged it with signing! For example, the well-known childhood game of "Operator" (see p. 161), in which children pass a message around the circle by whispering into one another's ears, can become a sign game that teaches new vocabulary and ASL sentence structure, while encouraging children to practice making signs. This game requires no materials and can be played anywhere, at any time.

INCLUDE ALL TEACHERS
AND STAFF MEMBERS

Sign language learning becomes more meaningful when all adults involved as instructors in a program are using it. Using ASL can become a significant part of your classroom "culture," and the participation of all members of the group is beneficial.

Adults learning the language along with the children can become a valuable teaching tool. It models excitement in learning new skills and acceptance of the inevitable mistakes you will make as you explore the language together. It shows the children that we are lifelong learners and we don't know everything! Moreover, if you do have children or families who are deaf in your program, it can teach the children a powerful lesson about respect and inclusiveness.

There are many demands placed upon us as early childhood educators, and some of your support staff may not see the value in using sign language with hearing children, or be willing to learn and implement "yet another" method of instruction. In our experience, however, when we use sign language with our students, and our colleagues begin to see the obvious benefits of integrating ASL in an early childhood classroom, they become eager participants.

SHARE WITH FAMILIES

The children in your early childhood classroom will without a doubt be the most willing and enthusiastic participants in the adventure of learning ASL. They love being able to move while learning and are captivated by the symbolic, visual nature of the language. Children feel proud and self-confident with their sign language skills and enjoy knowing a "secret" language that their families may not be familiar with. They inevitably bring their learning home and begin sharing ASL signs with their family members.

Feedback from families about their children's learning sign language at school is overwhelmingly positive. Parents and caregivers are thrilled that their child is learning a second language, increasing their awareness of diversity, and excited about learning. Families regularly report that their children teach them sign language at home and that they feel their child's self-confidence is improved by knowing ASL. They tell us that while at home, their children play the sign language games they learned at school and perform songs with signing. Parents frequently ask us to show them certain ASL words, phrases, or songs, so they can reinforce the language at home.

To promote this home-school learning connection, it is important to keep your families informed about the sign language curriculum. Early in the year you can send home a letter that explains the purpose, methods, and benefits of teaching ASL to hearing children (see p. 191 for a sample letter). In addition, it is helpful to print monthly packets with photocopies from your ASL dictionary of the vocabulary your students are learning. Send these packets home with your students, along with paper copies of photos of the children and teachers signing in class.

Most of all, don't forget to invite the families in your program to come into the classroom and see sign language in action! Whether they are spending some time volunteering on a regular school day, or invited to view a special performance that includes sign language, the families of your students will be pleased and amazed at how learning ASL impacts their child's education.

RELAX!

Don't worry about making mistakes. The guiding principles we present in this chapter are not unbreakable laws and the "sign language police" will not show up in your classroom to scold you! Use these ideas to guide your instruction and help you create and direct sign language activities that are enjoyable and meaningful.

It's Raining, It's Pouring

Try singing the lyrics to this familiar children's
song, adding the signs below.

It's raining, it's pouring,
The old man is snoring.
He bumped his head and he went to bed
and he couldn't get up in the morning.

SIGNS FOR "IT'S RAINING, IT'S POURING"

Rain

First you show the sign for water ("W" hand taps lips
with index finger), then both hands in "5" shape move
down wiggling (representing the rain drops).

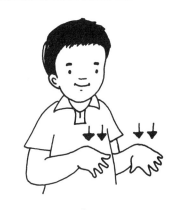

Pouring

Same as raining, just faster and harder.

Old

Make a fist below your chin and pull hand
downward like stroking a beard.

Man

With open hand, touch thumb to
forehead and then to chest.

Snoring

With your extended right index finger placed under your nose, pull hand away with a little flutter like the sound of snoring.

Bump

Right hand bumps into left hand.

Bed

Tilt head to one side with cheek resting in palm.

Not

The right thumb is tucked under the chin and pulled forward.

Awake

Pinch your index finger and thumb together at both sides of your face next to your eyes. As the fingers open, so do your eyes.

Morning

Right arm flat in front with left arm lying on top. Right arm with open hand rises to upright position (sun rising in the sky).

TEACHING AND LEARNING

ABOUT AMERICAN SIGN LANGUAGE AND DEAF CULTURE

Teaching children that American Sign Language is a unique and beautiful language used by many people who are deaf is one of the most important guiding principles of our sign language program. We want our hearing students to learn about deafness and Deaf culture, but as hearing teachers, addressing these issues in a responsible and sensitive manner can be difficult. This chapter explores the various resources, methods, lessons, and ideas that you can use to ensure that your sign language program is respectful to Deaf language and culture.

WHY TEACH ABOUT DEAFNESS AND DEAF CULTURE?

Including ASL in your program can help introduce your students to another culture and community. It will encourage young children to appreciate and accept differences between people. We know most early childhood teachers value anti-bias practice and strive to help young children understand diversity. A parent involved in our program who is deaf shared with us his thoughts on why learning about people who are deaf is beneficial to young children:

The experience of learning about another culture and their customs helps broaden young children's worlds and make them less self-centered. They realize there are other people, other values, other ideas, other identities. So when you teach sign language, you're introducing another culture, another value system. (B. Seago, 11/19/02, personal communication)

Including information about people who actually use sign language every day as a primary way to communicate will make the learning more meaningful for your students. ASL is the third most commonly used language in the United States today. People everywhere use sign language, many in your own community and probably even in your school. Teaching sign language to hearing children can help break down barriers between deaf and hearing people and increase understanding of Deaf culture. As we add signing to our work with young children, ASL use will increase. People who are deaf will benefit when more hearing people can communicate with them. People who are hearing will benefit from knowing another language and experiencing the unique cultural perspective of deaf people. Everyone wins!

LEARNING ABOUT DEAF CULTURE

Teachers who wish to share sign language with their hearing students or in their integrated deaf/hearing classrooms must know something about Deaf history and culture. After reading chapter 1 of this book, you already have a head start in understanding what Deaf culture means. You learned about another view of deafness—one that does not define it as a defect or disease to be cured. Rather, people who are deaf can be part of a unique community with a shared identity, history, and language. You know the critical connection ASL has to the Deaf community and the ongoing controversy surrounding its use in Deaf education. To learn even more about Deaf culture and the history of ASL and Deaf education, we recommend these three methods: read more about deaf people and Deaf culture, interact with people who are deaf, and include people who are deaf in your program.

Further Reading

There are many outstanding books by both deaf and hearing authors that explore the topic of deafness and the idea that deaf people can form a unique minority group (see "Resources" on page 193 for more suggested reading). We recommend two books about this topic for you to explore. They are *Seeing Voices: A Journey in the World of the Deaf* by Oliver Sacks (1989) and *The Mask of Benevolence: Disabling the Deaf Community* by Harlan Lane (1992). Both of these nonfiction works read like novels and explore in-depth Deaf history and the development of American Sign Language and Deaf culture. They are compelling stories and will no doubt influence your work as you teach and learn ASL with young hearing children.

Interact with People Who Are Deaf

The best way to learn about the culture of people who are deaf is to meet and interact with deaf people! No doubt there are people in your community who are hard of hearing or deaf. We both live in small, rural areas and still have had many interactions with people who are deaf and hearing people who are part of the Deaf community

for various reasons. We know hearing adults who grew up with deaf parents, hearing people who are fluent signers, deaf and hearing married couples, and people who work as ASL interpreters. We have grown up with friends who are deaf, had deaf students in our classrooms, and taught hearing students that have deaf family members. Here are some ways to locate and meet people in the Deaf community in your area:

- **Find a community education American Sign Language course.** Many times these classes are taught by native signers (someone who may be either deaf or hearing, but grew up using ASL).

- **Locate public school programs for deaf and hard-of-hearing students.** Here you can meet children and adults who are deaf and learn from other teachers working with these students.

- **Contact a Deaf school.** Deaf schools often present another opportunity to meet deaf children and adults. In addition, Deaf schools are often the Deaf "cultural hub" and will have information on Deaf community events in your area, such as ASL conversation dinners, conferences, or classes.

- **Talk to your colleagues, family, and friends.** It is very likely that someone you work with or someone in your extended community knows a deaf or hard-of-hearing person who would be willing to help you learn more about ASL and Deaf culture.

You may be concerned about how you will communicate with people who are deaf when you first begin to interact with members of the Deaf community. First of all, understand that like hearing people, people who are deaf are unique individuals. They come from different family situations and educational backgrounds, and do not all feel the same connection to Deaf culture. In addition, there are varying degrees of deafness, from mild hearing loss to profound deafness (no ability to hear any sounds). Some people are born deaf and others may have lost their hearing later in life. Some do not acquire oral language, while others are able to speak. Finally, people with hearing loss or deafness will use different methods to communicate. They may use lipreading and speech, ASL or other sign languages, or a combination thereof.

It is more than likely that because you will be new to the use of ASL, your first interactions will be with deaf people who can lip-read and speak, or with hearing people who are fluent signers and may have family members or close friends who are deaf. In any case, if you are not sure what type of communication to use, just ask. There are also several available services that can accommodate deaf and hearing interactions, like TTY devices and phone relays for telephone conversations, pagers with text messaging, and sign language interpreters.

(A TTY is a device that is attached to a telephone and "rings" by flashing a light. People who are deaf can type messages on a keyboard that are then sent out over phone lines to another TTY. The messages appear on a screen. If you don't have a TTY, and you are trying to telephone a person who uses a TTY, you can call a TTY operator who will type the messages to be sent and read you the reply! This is called a TTY relay.)

Include People Who Are Deaf in Your Program

If you are lucky enough to befriend persons who are deaf or hearing persons who are fluent in ASL and familiar with Deaf culture, ask if they might be willing to help you with your new sign language curriculum. Tell them that you are interested in learning ASL and sharing it with your students and explain why you think the addition of ASL in your classroom will benefit everyone involved. You can begin by simply inviting them to your classroom to see what you are doing! The inclusion of people who are deaf is one of the best ways for you and your students to learn about Deaf culture.

Because each volunteer situation will be unique, we cannot give you specific details about how to implement this practice. However, we can share with you our experience of including members of the Deaf community in our program and how it has helped us with our understanding of what it means to be deaf and how to appropriately interact and communicate with deaf people.

Our experience with volunteers from the Deaf community includes having friends who are deaf come to class to play, eat lunch, and sign with our students, conversing with deaf parents about their experiences, and having a hearing parent who is a sign language interpreter in class once a week to introduce ASL activities and help correct our signing. These volunteers have shared with us their opinions about using sign language with hearing populations and made themselves available to us as resources to enhance the cultural appropriateness of the sign language program.

The father of one of our students who is deaf told us how he felt about the inclusion of Deaf community members in the program:

> I strongly encourage any program that uses ASL to have experienced deaf people involved. It's really valuable. I can't stress it enough! Deaf people are the best ambassadors to that world, to teach hearing people. Bring in that deaf person and that person is now an extension of their world in their little safe environment. So I'm a strong advocate. Anytime you have the opportunity to have deaf people involved, bring them in. (B. Seago, personal communication, 11/19/02)

We agree and feel that it is very important to have someone who is aware of Deaf culture involved in helping you develop your curriculum. It will help you practice your signing, and teach ASL in a more meaningful way.

Here are a few examples of ways that volunteers in our programs have helped us understand Deaf language and culture:

- **Correcting our signing.** A volunteer who was a sign language interpreter would come to school once a week and observe our circle time sign language activities. She would show us new signs and help us make the signs correctly if we were making mistakes. For example, we were doing the sign for "talk" as we learned it from an ASL dictionary. It shows the signer with one finger on each side of the mouth moving front and back. She corrected us, saying that that sign indicates two people talking together, but that four fingers on one hand in front of your mouth means one person "talking."

- **Showing us appropriate ways to get the children's attention.** To stop the activity in the classroom and get the children's attention, we would often ring a bell. One day, while a deaf volunteer was working with us, we did this and he just looked at us like we were crazy! He then walked over to the light switch and switched the lights on and off a few times. He explained that in a classroom with deaf children, this is what they would do, and it works equally well with hearing kids. In addition, during circle time activities we would often sign "watch me" to get the children to focus on us. We learned that it is appropriate to bang on the floor with your open hand to grab the children's attention to refocus.

- **Understanding sign names.** We have seen in other sign language curriculum books an activity that involves the children choosing for themselves a "sign name." They are instructed to use the manual letter for the first letter in their name, along with a sign that represents something about themselves. For example, making the manual letter "K" for Kirsten, with the sign for "teacher." We were told by our friends who are deaf that this is a very inappropriate activity for hearing people to be doing. Sign names are an intimate part of Deaf culture, and are only to be given by a deaf person. In our program, we use finger spelling to indicate children's names.

- **Discussing accommodation devices.** While signing a finger play about "monkeys jumping on the bed" one day, we realized that when "mama calls the doctor," she needs to use a TTY device instead of a telephone! This sparked a discussion of TTYs and how they are used.

These are just some of the many ways volunteers from the Deaf community have helped us make our sign language program meaningful and appropriate. We are continually learning more each year as we include deaf people in our schools as advisors, observers, mentors, and friends!

TEACHING ABOUT DEAF CULTURE

Another guiding principle of this sign language curriculum is that early childhood teachers should start simply integrating signing into daily classroom activities, without a big introduction of what ASL is and why you all are going to learn it. Remember— just do it! Most children will come to regard signing as a normal way to communicate at school and probably think that all teachers "talk with their hands"! However, after a few weeks it is important to begin sharing with the children what sign language is and teaching them about deaf people who use ASL every day to communicate their feelings, thoughts, and opinions. Two good ways to start introducing children to deafness and Deaf culture are to use children's books and to facilitate relationships between children and people who are deaf.

Use Children's Books

The following is a list of children's books that you can use to begin discussing this topic with your young hearing students. We have found these books, which feature children who are deaf, to be especially useful in helping hearing children relate to and understand what it may be like to be hard of hearing or deaf. They sensitively explore differences in ways that young children can understand. In addition, they provide useful information about Deaf cultural norms.

We recommend the following children's books:

- *I'm Deaf and It's O.K.* (Aseltine, Mueller & Tait, 1986). This story is about a boy who wears hearing aids and goes to a special school with other deaf and hard-of-hearing children. He becomes angry when he realizes that he will always need his hearing aids, but with the help of an older deaf boy, he realizes that he can do many things with his life even though he wears hearing aids. This book is best read in sections, as it is a bit long for very young children.

- *I Have a Sister, My Sister Is Deaf* (Peterson, 1977). This story is told from the perspective of an older sister about how her five-year-old deaf sister experiences the world and the special relationship they share. You can discuss with your students how the sister who is deaf can "feel" sounds, how the hearing sister gets her deaf sister's attention, and why the little girl did not like her older sister wearing big dark sunglasses. Also, because the deaf child in this book is about the same age as the children in your program, you can talk about the similarities among them. (She likes to pet cats, go to school, and ride on a swing!)

- *Dad and Me in the Morning* (Lakin, 1994). This is a beautifully illustrated book about a young boy who is deaf and a special morning he spends watching the sunrise with his dad. It also explores different ways children who are deaf may communicate through sign language, facial expression, voice, and speech reading.

- *Moses Goes to School* (Millman, 2000). This book, about a boy who attends a public school for deaf children, emphasizes the use of ASL and demonstrates how it is different from spoken English. Moses and all of his classmates are deaf or hard of hearing, and they all use ASL to communicate with each other, the teachers (some of whom are deaf), and even the crossing guards (who are hearing). The book includes illustrations for ASL words and phrases and some song lyrics. Other titles by this same author include *Moses Goes to a Concert* (2002), *Moses Goes to the Circus* (2003), and *Moses Sees a Play* (2004). All four are wonderful books that present deafness and the use of American Sign Language in positive ways. They also include relevant examples of Deaf life, like the use of TTY devices, ASL storytelling, interactions with hearing people, and how people who are deaf can and do enjoy entertainment events.

Facilitate Relationships between Children and People Who Are Deaf

Just as interaction with people who are deaf can benefit hearing teachers wanting to learn ASL and understand Deaf culture, young hearing children benefit greatly from interacting with other children or adults who are hard of hearing or deaf. As a teacher, you can facilitate these relationships in several ways.

- **Include deaf children or deaf family members.** Obviously if you have children or family members who are deaf involved in your program, this creates a wonderful opportunity to learn about Deaf culture. Encourage participation from family members or friends of deaf or hard-of-hearing students. As your students learn more ASL, invite them into the classroom to sign with you.

- **Partner with a class at a Deaf school.** There are many ways to interact with children at another school for students who are deaf. Your children can create videos to send to them in which they sign their names and show them their classroom activities. Teachers can help the children send e-mail to one another, telling about their families, pets, and what they like to do for fun. In addition, once you have built a familiar relationship, you can take a field trip to visit the school, invite the students to visit your classroom, or travel together to see a play by a local Deaf theater group.

- **Encourage classroom volunteers.** Invite deaf people into your classroom whenever you can. It is the single most effective way for your children to understand deafness and begin to relate to people with different abilities. Our experience with this has been overwhelmingly positive. It is a joy to watch young hearing children signing with deaf adults and to see their eyes light up when they are understood. They learn so much about interacting with deaf people, like they have to tap the person who is deaf to get their attention, and that deaf people can be quite loud!

LEARNING AMERICAN SIGN LANGUAGE

In any culture, a shared language is a critical part of what binds a group of people together. For people who are deaf and who consider themselves members of the Deaf culture, their native language is American Sign Language. When we consider using ASL with young hearing children to achieve various benefits, it is important that we respect the language and use it correctly. Again, speaking with a volunteer who is deaf helped us to understand why this is important:

First of all, it shows respect for our Deaf culture, respect for our language, and allows us to show our values and our pride, our identity. It's recognition. I mean if you look at it from a cultural view, rather than a pathological view, it really does. Because if you're learning ASL, it's like learning the language of another culture. But when you're learning SEE (Signed Exact English), you're not learning a language. You're learning a sign system to represent English that was created by someone outside Deaf culture. Because it was invented by a hearing person. (B. Seago, personal communication, 11/20/02)

We strongly advocate the use of ASL and know through experience that it is an engaging and easy-to-learn language for young hearing children (and adults)!

You will not need to know a lot of ASL before you can start integrating it into your work with hearing preschoolers. When we started, we knew only a few signs for children's songs and some "classroom management" signs. We just kept learning vocabulary and then teaching it to our students as we went along. All it takes is the enthusiasm to try something new and the willingness to take risks and make mistakes.

Here are some basic tips to help you begin learning the beautiful language of American Sign:

- Start by getting a good American Sign Language dictionary (see our resource list for suggestions).

- Learn the manual alphabet—the hand shapes that represent letters.

- Do not make up signs. If you don't know a sign, look it up or ask someone for help.

- Attend an ASL class through your local community education center.

- Check out ASL videos from your local library.

- Hang out with deaf people!

- Don't worry about being perfect. There are variations on how people sign just as there are variations on how people speak.

- ASL is a visual language, unlike spoken English, which uses sound.

- Like sentences in any foreign language, ASL sentences are not a word-for-word translation of English. ASL sentences use different word order, grammar, and syntax than English ones do.

- ASL uses hand shape (how you form your hand), location (where the hand is placed), and movement (how the hand moves) to form signs.

- ASL uses a lot of facial expression to communicate.

- Eye contact is very important when communicating with someone in ASL.

As you use American Sign Language more in your classroom, you will grow in your abilities and confidence, just as the children will. Again, deaf volunteers in your classroom can be of great assistance for beginning ASL learners. Before we began working with members of the Deaf community, we were mainly using Signed English with our students. Because we are hearing women and were primarily working with hearing children, it was easier to do it this way. Our deaf friends and advisors helped to show us how to use ASL sentence structure and think of the language as expressing visual concepts, instead of translating English word for word.

For example, one October we were going over vocabulary for our fall sign language Basket Game and came to the sign for "trick or treat." We were using two different signs, one for "trick" and one for "candy." A volunteer who is an ASL interpreter showed us a completely different sign for "trick or treat" that involved pretending to knock on a door while sticking your tongue in and out. She reminded us that ASL is about expressing visual ideas. She also helped us understand the structure of ASL sentences by introducing games with ASL phrases. We often played "I Spy" (see p. 122) and she showed us that instead of signing "I spy with my eye something red," it was correct in ASL to sign, "Red, I see."

Teaching ASL to Young Hearing Children

Many educators teaching sign language to hearing children use Signed English because they believe it is easier for hearing people to learn. In addition, they may feel it is more developmentally appropriate for young hearing children, still learning spoken language, to learn a second language that follows the same structure that English does. Because of our experience using correct American Sign Language with young hearing children, reading about the history of ASL, and talking to deaf people about its importance to their culture, we believe that if a hearing teacher uses sign language with her hearing students, it should be ASL.

We understand the importance of teaching young hearing children to understand that "ASL is not English" and we have come up with strategies to help you illustrate the differences to children. For example, you can use a simple reading lesson to demonstrate the difference in word order between ASL and English. Part of our reading program involves the children's reading short words by sounding out the letters, then putting the words together to form short, simple sentences. We integrate ASL into this lesson by finger spelling the words, signing the words, and signing the sentence. When we read the sentences, we do it in English and in ASL. We tell them, "This is English: 'I can run.' But in American Sign Language we sign: 'Run, I can.' We can say it both ways: 'I can run. Run, I can.'"

In addition, you can teach the children to count up to the number ten in ASL (see p. 147). Most children this age know how to count on their fingers, but in ASL numbers are shown using only one hand and in different configurations than the children are familiar with. For example, ASL for the number six is the forefinger and thumb touching, with the remaining three fingers up. This provides a great opportunity to illustrate the fact that ASL and English are different languages. It is a concrete representation of the different languages.

Another unique characteristic of American Sign Language is that the signs represent visual concepts and are not word-for-word translations of English. This idea can be demonstrated by playing the game "Mother, May I?" (see p. 70) in ASL.

The children are told by the signer ("mother") how to move closer to her. For example, they are told to hop three steps, jump two jumps, or slide four slides. When playing this game using sign language, if the signer wanted the children to take three small steps, he would not sign "three," and then "small" and then "step." Instead he would make the sign for "three" and then "walk" (both hands, palms down in front of the body and moving like feet walking), but his hands would be in very close to his body and only moving slightly up and down, to indicate the concept of "small."

A volunteer in the program who is deaf suggested to us another method to get the children to understand American Sign Language. He encouraged us to read the children familiar stories and then "act them out" in ASL. Because there is no written form of ASL, sign language storytelling is a traditional part of Deaf culture. It is considered by many people who are deaf as an art form, and all over the world there are Deaf theater groups that perform many different types of plays. If you ever get the chance to see one of these ASL theater shows, you will be awed by the power and beauty of the performance.

In our classrooms, we have learned to sign several stories and found it to be a very powerful tool for the children to understand the visual language of ASL. Of course, you'll need to know enough ASL to communicate the basic message of the story to the children. But we were able to do it and we are nowhere near fluent, so you can too! It is a very worthwhile activity. The children will watch you intently and be completely still and silent.

If you do not feel confident enough in your signing skills to do this activity, there are several good videos of stories told in ASL. Try *Sign-Me-A-Story* by Linda Bove, *ASL Fairy Tales I & II* by Paul Chamberlain, or something from the *Visual Tales* series by Billy Seago. Additional resources for teaching children about ASL include the books *The Handmade Alphabet* and *The Handmade Counting Book* by Laura Rankin. There are many sign language storybooks for children, but many of them use Signed English, so read descriptions carefully.

Watching stories told through ASL on videotapes and in books are effective ways to expose young children to true ASL. But seeing a real person sign fluently to communicate is the most effective and dramatic teaching tool there is. Here again is where your relationships with people who are deaf and willing to help you can be a great benefit to you and your young hearing students.

In our experience, as the school year progresses and the children learn more signing vocabulary, we encourage the volunteers to take a more prominent role during their visits by leading the children in a new game or sign language activity. This is a wonderful experience for the children because our signing friends tend to use their voices much less than we hearing folks. It is great to watch them use their bodies and get the children's attention through movement and through sign language.

One game that was introduced to the children by a volunteer was called "Funny Face" (see p. 54). ASL uses a lot of facial expression and this activity helps the children practice making different movements with their facial muscles. The expressions are quite animated and the exercise helps children warm up to using their bodies to communicate ideas and feelings.

Finally, an important goal for the program and a meaningful way to be respectful to the Deaf culture when using sign language as hearing people is teaching the children to use ASL as a way to communicate. As opposed to just learning to sign songs and vocabulary words, we want the children to be competent enough signers that they could communicate in ASL with people who are deaf. Integrating signing into your daily activities like calendar, snack time, stories, and dramatic play makes the ASL learning ongoing and meaningful.

Another piece of the sign language curriculum that we have developed is called "Sign Times" (see p. 27). As the children acquire a substantial ASL vocabulary (usually after a few months), you can begin to set aside time during the day where you and the children try to communicate only in ASL. Start with short time periods, usually just five minutes, and if you have taught your children the "Snack Signs" (see p. 108), snack or lunch time is a great time to begin this "no voice" activity.

At first you will probably see the children making faces and doing a lot of pointing and gesturing. They will need a lot of teacher help and encouragement to use the signs they know. As your school year progresses and your ASL vocabulary increases, you will find they can sign for longer and longer periods of time. Try it at different times of the day also, and remember, they don't have to be silent during this time! It's okay to laugh and make noise. "Sign Times" just gives you all an opportunity to use the ASL you are learning for real communication.

Using the ideas and activities presented in this chapter will help make your sign language curriculum culturally appropriate and meaningful. You and your students have the opportunity to discover a rich and vibrant culture and learn the beautiful visual language of American Sign. Your students will learn about a diverse group of people with different abilities and challenges. If you have deaf or hard-of-hearing students, family, or staff members in your program, teaching and learning about ASL and Deaf culture models respect and demonstrates the value of inclusiveness.

SIGN TIME

To help you and the children experience ASL, you can set aside blocks of time during the school day when the only communication is with sign language. Start with five minutes at snack time when everyone is together. These "sign times" can also help calm the classroom if the noise level gets too loud.

GOALS

- To experience communicating without words
- To practice sign language vocabulary
- To learn new signs
- To have children see the teachers signing to one another

MATERIALS

None

PROCEDURE

This lesson can be started a few months into the school year, after the children have mastered several signs. Talk about it at circle time, telling the children that you are all going to practice communicating only in ASL. Help them think of some signs or sign language phrases they might need to know. For example, if you're doing "Sign Time" at snack, useful signs might include "more," "finished," "thank you," and "please."

"Sign Time" works well when the whole group is together, for example, at snack or lunch time. The teachers need to take the lead and set an example for using sign language to communicate. Some children whisper, some children make faces and point or gesture to communicate. This is okay at the beginning, but when you see this, try to figure out what they are trying to communicate and show them how to do it in ASL.

NOTE

By observing what the children do during these blocks of time, you can see which signs they know well and can use to communicate and where they need more help. Notice who is doing the signing, who just sits quietly, and those who can't "lock their voices"!

FOLLOW-UP

"Sign Time" can continue throughout the year. Try it during different times of your day, like center time or during an art activity. As the children become more competent signers, you can try doing no voices for expanded amounts of time.

DEAF CULTURE SIGNS

American Sign Language

Make both hands in the "A" shape. Rotate hands (circling) toward the body alternately, then make two "L" hands and move them out toward the sides of the body.

Deaf

The tip of the extended right index finger touches first your right ear and then your closed lips.

Hearing

Your right index finger, pointing left, makes small circles under your lower lip. This sign comes from words pouring out of the mouth.

Sign

Two "D" hands circling in front of you.

Teletypewriter

Hold your right hand in the "Y" shape, placing your little finger by your mouth and your thumb by your ear, then mime using a typewriter (telephone + typewriter).

CHAPTER 5

AMERICAN SIGN LANGUAGE

IN AN EARLY CHILDHOOD LITERACY PROGRAM

As you read in chapter 2, research shows that an early childhood literacy program that includes signing as an additional tool to help children understand letters, sounds, and words provides several advantages. This chapter explains these benefits and describes activities and methods that can help you, as an early childhood educator, integrate ASL into your reading and writing curriculum.

WHY IT WORKS

Signing with young hearing children works to enhance early literacy skills for these reasons:

- Signing engages children in literacy activities.

- Signing allows children to use multiple senses to learn new information.

- The signs children will learn "look" like the letters and words you want to teach them.

- Creating signs helps children connect concrete objects to abstract concepts.

- Signing increases young children's confidence to learn new skills.

Engagement

American Sign Language is very interesting to young children and is a highly motivating form of instruction. Using sign language during reading and writing activities helps "hook" the children into your instruction. Whether you are singing the ABC song and signing the letters, or signing various words from a children's book, your students will be watching you intently, focused on your every move. This intense engagement and focus helps young children be ready to learn new skills and information.

Multisensory Process

Teaching early literacy skills in different ways benefits young hearing children. Including American Sign Language when you teach letters of the alphabet, sounds, and words gives children another way to understand them. They not only see the letters with their eyes and hear the sounds with their ears, but they also physically create the letters and words with their bodies.

This type of teaching addresses all learning styles and provides young children with multiple ways to remember information. We have found that our students very frequently use the signs to help them remember letter names, sounds, and words. In addition, children with speech disabilities who may not be able to pronounce sounds and words can still demonstrate their understanding of the alphabet with sign language.

Create "Pictures" of Letters and Words

Many ASL signs, including the sign language alphabet, look like their meanings. For example, the letter "y" is formed by holding up the thumb and pinky of one hand, the sign for "car" is two hands grasping an imaginary steering wheel, and to sign "milk" you basically pretend to milk a cow! This "iconicity" really helps children understand and remember letters and words. The signs provide a visual and physical memory in their minds.

Bridge Concrete to Abstract

Additional cues can help children understand the alphabet and words. Signing creates a bridge between concrete objects and the abstract symbols (letters and words) that represent the objects. For example, the children see a cat, they hear you say the word "cat," you show them how to stroke an imaginary pair of whiskers on their face (the sign for "cat"), and then they see the word "cat" on paper. The addition of sign language provides another meaningful step between the object and the word that represents the object.

Build Confidence

When you add ASL to your literacy activities, the children in your classrooms will learn the alphabet names and sounds earlier and understand and recognize more vocabulary words. While these early literacy skills are important steps in creating successful readers and writers, signing provides another valuable benefit. Including ASL in your program increases the enjoyment of reading and writing activities for your students. They feel confident in their new skills, are excited about learning language, and are enthusiastic to confront new academic challenges.

HOW TO INCLUDE ASL IN AN EARLY CHILDHOOD LITERACY PROGRAM

One of the many wonderful things about including American Sign Language in an early childhood classroom is that you don't have to reinvent your program to make it effective. There are many ways to teach literacy skills to young children, and ASL can be easily integrated into your existing language activities. The key is to remember the multisensory process of seeing, saying, signing, and reading. The following section lists the methods we have used to include signing in an early childhood literacy program.

Learning the Alphabet

You can easily incorporate ASL into your teaching of the alphabet and letter sounds using five common early childhood curriculum strategies: the ABC song, finger spelling, the Basket Game, "Show and Tell," and alphabet puzzles and games.

THE ABC SONG

This is a great place to start learning ASL and teaching early literacy skills like the names of the letters. Sing the ABC song slowly, while you make the alphabet signs (see p. 34) with your hand for the children to see. You can have helpers assist the children with forming the letters while they watch you. Practice the ABC song several times and continue throughout the school year. We also sing this song making the sounds (aaa, buh, cuh, duh) instead of saying the names of letters while we sign them. It is also helpful to hang a poster of the ASL finger alphabet for you and the children to refer to.

FINGER SPELLING

After a few days of practicing singing and signing your ABCs, you can begin finger spelling (spelling words with the letter signs). We usually start with the children's names and finger spell to dismiss them. It does not take very long before they are confidently recognizing their name and their classmates' names in ASL.

BASKET GAME

In this version of the Basket Game, use magnet, wood, or plastic letters, or alphabet flash cards for the objects in the basket. Introduce only half the letters at a time. We start with the letters A through M. Show the children the letter as you make the sign. Have them make the sign back to you. Lay out the letters on the floor and call on students to pick up the one you sign to them. The children enjoy playing this game as a large group and also on their own with friends. Remember to sign "good job" when they get the right one, and "again" if they did not. If they need help you can sign "forget?"

"SHOW AND TELL"

Turn your "Show and Tell" into a literacy activity with sign language by asking the children in your class to bring in objects from home hidden in paper sacks with the first letter of the object written on the front. As you go around the circle, read the letter on each bag out loud, and make the sound with your voice as you form the sign with your hand. Ask the children to do it too. Then the children get a chance to guess what is in the bag. If you know the sign for the word they are guessing, show them. For example, a child brings in a bag with the letter "b" on it. The children guess, "Is it a baby?" (you show the sign for baby), "Is it a book?" (you show the sign for book). You might want to have an ASL dictionary handy for this activity to quickly look up signs you don't know.

PUZZLES AND BOARD GAMES

There are a variety of alphabet puzzles and games available for early childhood teachers, and sign language can be included in any one of them. We frequently played with small groups of children using a wooden alphabet puzzle. After taking apart the puzzle, the teacher would sign a letter to the children and they would put the correct letter back. After a few times the children enjoyed doing this without the teacher and just with a partner or a few friends.

Letter or word bingo games are also perfect for including ASL signs. Just follow the regular rules of the game, but sign the letters or words instead of calling them out. To be Deaf-culturally appro-priate, we also teach our kids to stomp their feet on the floor and wave their hands in the air instead of shouting "bingo!"

As with the ABC song, while playing these games you can switch from using the names of the letters to making their sounds instead.

Learning Words

Many of the techniques you already use to help children combine letters into short words can be adapted to include the use of ASL. Here are four of them to get you started: classroom print, phonics lessons, guess the word, and word mix-up.

CLASSROOM PRINT

Many early childhood teachers label objects in their classrooms (such as tables, doors, chairs, books, or blocks) in print for the children to see what the words look like. You can add to their understanding of this "environmental print" by posting ASL signs for these words as well. Use these labels for your center areas, objects in the classroom, calendar words, and supplies. Children's names can also be printed in the American Sign Language alphabet on cubbies, attendance lists, or classroom job lists. You can use copies of the illustrations in this book, in an ASL dictionary, or on sign language flash cards.

PHONICS LESSONS

Learning to recognize phonemes (letter sounds) is an important early literacy skill. While we do not expect very young children to master these skills, many are quite capable and eager to try. The addition of ASL when teaching letter sounds makes this learning even more accessible.

This activity will probably work best with the older children in your group (four- to six-year-olds) and is most effectively done in small groups (five children or fewer). Using magnet letters, alphabet flash cards, or a whiteboard or chalkboard, you can show the children letters while making the sounds and signs.

Then start putting letters together to form small words and try sounding them out with the children. For example, write "m," make the sound, and show the sign. Do the same with "o" and then "p." Then go back and point to the letters one at a time a little more quickly, saying and signing at the same time ("mmm, ahhh, puh, MOP!"). When the children figure out the word, it is important to show them the sign for that word also, so they are not just finger spelling it. Ask them to finger spell as they say the sounds, and then say the word with the sign.

As their reading vocabulary increases, try doing this activity with short sentences. It is a great way to teach about the different structures of ASL and English. They can read a sentence like "I see the dog" in English and you can tell them (and sign) in ASL it would be "dog, I see."

GUESS THE WORD

In this game, children work together as a team to solve a word puzzle before the teacher finishes drawing a picture of the word. You will need a whiteboard or chalkboard to work on. Think of a word that you want the children to guess and draw a blank line for each letter in the word. Use short (three- to six-letter), simple words that do not contain silent sounds. Have the children sign to you letters they think are in the word. If they guess correctly, write the letter in the correct blank. If the letter they guess is not in the word, record it off to the side and draw a small part of the picture. As the picture of the object emerges, the children's guesses will be more accurate. You can even ask them to tell you "where" in the word they think the letter belongs. This is a great game for children of all skill levels. All children can guess and feel that they are an important part of the team. The vocabulary words you use can even match your themes of study!

WORD MIX-UP

This game helps children understand about letter order within words and the idea that print goes from left to right. Using the same materials as for the phonics and guessing word games, make words for the children to see, but mix up the letters. You need to use words that the children know the sign for because the idea is for the children to sign you the word when you've got it in the correct order. For example, you write the word "sun" as "usn" or "nus" and when they see it as "sun" their hands go up, making the sign for "sun." You can then have

them finger spell, say the sounds, say the word, and make the sign ("ssss, uuh, nnn, SUN!").

Using Children's Literature

We know that reading with young children is probably the best way of enhancing early literacy learning. There are many ways you can include ASL while exploring children's books with your students.

SIGNING STORIES

Books with repetitive words and phrases are great for learning new vocabulary. We use books like *The Very Hungry Caterpillar* (Carle, 1969) and sign the recurring phrases as we say them out loud.

You can also choose books about whatever theme you are exploring in your classroom to reinforce new vocabulary words. As you read the books, sign the key words while you say them or even try just signing them without your voice and have the children guess what the word is. They love this activity and will listen and watch you intently to try and anticipate the next sign.

In addition, acting out whole stories with sign language is great fun and a wonderful way for children to experience the language of ASL. After reading a story several times that the children enjoy, and signing key vocabulary and phrases, try just signing as much of the story as you can without speaking. It is wonderful to see how much you can communicate with just your body, and the children will really start making connections between the story, the signs, and the printed words.

BIG BOOKS AND CHART POEMS

Big books (large books with large print) and chart poems (poems or songs printed on large lined paper) can be used to reinforce the connection between the spoken words of a story or poem, the signs, and the text. By placing these large print texts where they can be shared with a group of children, you can help children recognize the printed words that represent the spoken words, visual objects, and signs you are using. For example, copy the text of *Five Little Pumpkins* (Young, 1995) on large chart paper and learn to sign the key words like pumpkin, gate, late, run, and fun. Then ask the children to locate in the text words that you sign to them.

Writing

Early reading and writing learning are connected, and just as ASL can be included in reading activities, you can incorporate signing into early childhood experiences with writing. In our program we do a combination of teacher-modeled writing with young children and independent writing by the children using "invented" spelling. (The children listen for sounds in words and write down what they hear.)

GROUP WRITING

Every day in our classrooms we give one child the job of telling us a bit of "news" that we record on large chart paper. We do this as a whole group, usually at our morning circle time. The teacher does the writing, but asks the children for help remembering what letters make certain sounds. For example, if Abby says her news is "Abby is going to her grandma's house," you can first say, "How do you spell Abby?" Then with the children you finger spell and say the letters in her name. For the word "grandma" or "house" you can say the word slowly, listening for letter sounds and ask, "What is that sound?" The children will sign or say the letter for you to write. You can also use this group writing activity to record a class field trip, list observations from a nature walk, or create your own class books. Whenever you do activities that include letter names and sounds, just add signing too!

INDEPENDENT WRITING

When young children are ready to write on their own, knowing the signs for letters can be a useful tool to help them remember what sounds each letter makes. Whether writing in journals, labeling pictures, writing notes to friends or the teacher, or recording a story, children who know sign language will use this skill to help them sound out and spell words. You can help them by slowly repeating the words they want to write and isolating sounds. Show them the sign for the letters they are trying to write and have the English alphabet available for them to see.

Including American Sign Language in your early childhood literacy program is easy! You can use the ideas described in this chapter as well as add signing to what you are already doing. As you start signing with your language activities, you will soon see the advantages to this kind of instruction. Your students will be enthusiastic language learners, understanding letters and sounds, exploring writing, and enjoying books in ways they never have before.

LITERACY SIGNS

The signs on the following pages are especially helpful in supporting early literacy in your program.

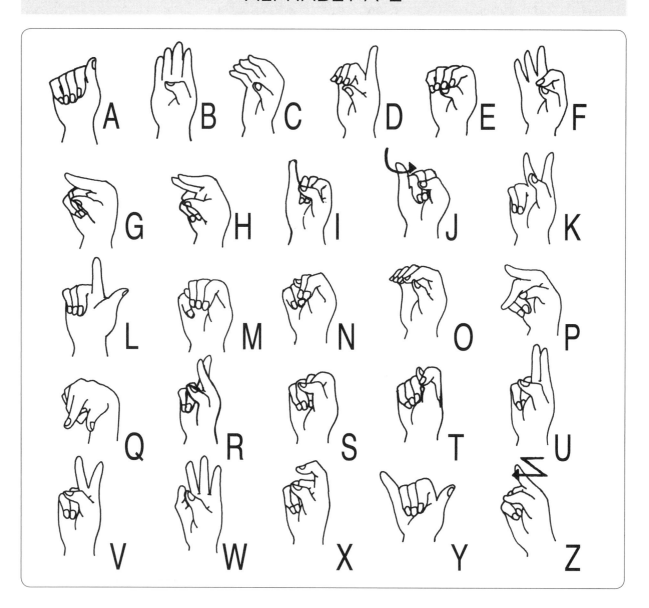

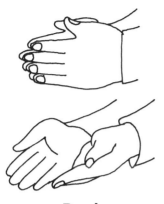

Book

Open and close both hands with little finger as the spine of the book.

Finger Spelling

Using your right hand, palm out, move from left to right with your fingers wiggling.

Read

Hold a right "V" hand in front of the left palm as if the left palm were a book and your "V" the eyes reading.

Sentence

Both hands in "F" position, with fingertips touching, move apart to either side in a wavy motion.

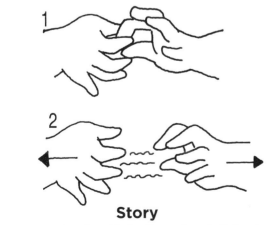

Story

Link your thumb and index fingers from both hands in "F" shape and pull them apart a few times.

Word

With left hand in "D" shape and right hand in "G" shape, tap left index finger with right index finger.

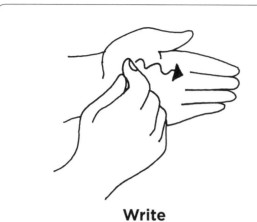

Write

Right hand holds thumb and index finger
pinched together as if grasping a pen and
writes on left open palm.

AMERICAN SIGN LANGUAGE

FOR CLASSROOM MANAGEMENT

As an educator, you know that how you manage your classroom environment is a critical part of a successful early childhood program. Classroom management includes how you set up your physical space, plan your daily schedule, create routines, and address the needs of diverse learners. You manage your classroom by how you handle transitions, teach social skills, model expectations, and redirect unwanted behaviors.

When teachers of young hearing children add American Sign Language to their classroom management strategies, they discover multiple benefits. Sign language can be used to influence the noise level of your classroom, help you communicate effectively with students, manage unwanted behavior, and build classroom community. This chapter describes different ways of including ASL in your classroom management plan and specific advantages of using these methods.

Including American Sign Language in your classroom management plan allows you to do the following:

- Engage your students

- Effectively redirect behavior

- Establish routines

- Ease transitions

- Address different learning styles

- Increase communication with children with special needs

- Create a common language in a multilingual classroom

- Help children understand and express feelings

- Calm the classroom

- Build community

ENGAGE YOUR STUDENTS

When we want to give directions to a group of children, or explain an activity, or teach a concept, we first need to get their attention. Sometimes with a group of wiggly young children, this can be a bit difficult! Sign language is extremely interesting to children, and when teachers use it, they find their students very engaged and focused. When you use ASL to communicate with hearing children, they are forced to look at you to get information. They make eye contact and notice facial expressions and are typically more motivated to "tune in" to what you are trying to tell them.

One effective strategy for using ASL to grab the attention of young children is to begin by using your voice and signing at the same time. Say, "If you can hear my voice, touch your head" while you make the signs for "hear," "voice," and "head." Keep doing this with different body parts and as the children focus more on you, slowly make your voice quieter, and then take it away all together. Once you have their attention this way, continue with your activity!

EFFECTIVELY REDIRECT BEHAVIOR

Including ASL in an early childhood classroom with hearing children is a powerful tool to help you redirect unwanted behavior. Children seem to respond better to the visual cues provided by signing than to verbal reminders. We all know how annoying it can be to repeat the same message over and over and start sounding like a "nag." By using sign language, we can grab their attention, make eye contact, use our facial expressions, and communicate our message quickly and effectively.

In addition, this kind of communication can eliminate the humiliation of "getting in trouble." If you sign something across the room to a child, you don't have to stop the whole class. It is just between you and the child. Signing to redirect behavior is quick and easy and does not take up as much classroom time for discipline. We have found that signing to children quietly about their behavior helps build a trusting relationship between the teacher and student. The children know they will not be embarrassed by everyone's hearing the teacher's voice reprimanding them.

Start right away introducing basic classroom management signs to the children in your class. Again, when you first begin you will want to use your voice and sign at the same time. We usually begin with "sit down," "walking feet," "quiet voice," "wait," "watch me," "yes," "no," "thank you," "stop," "come here," "forget?" (did you forget?), "remember," and "again." You can include any other words or phrases that you find yourself using often with your students. It takes a little time and modeling for the children to figure out this kind of communication. Practice getting close to the children and making the signs as you tell them with your voice what you want them to do.

Two signs we use often with our students are "finish" and "not friendly." We use "finish" to basically mean "cut it out!" and stop whatever behavior is happening. "Not friendly" is a powerful phrase to use with children when they are having trouble sharing or when they are arguing, pushing, or hitting. "Not friendly" really stops the behavior because children do not want to be viewed this way. If you make a grumpy, sad face while signing "not friendly," and then contrast that with a happy, smiling face with the sign for "friendly," the children really understand the message clearly.

ESTABLISH ROUTINES

Establishing classroom routines helps children feel secure and confident in their school environment. They know what to expect from day to day, and feel a sense of control and independence in their classroom. Teachers can use their voices with signs to introduce and implement classroom routines. It will not take long before your students will know what you are telling them when you use only ASL. You will be amazed at how motivated they are by this method of communication! The children will understand the ASL signs and know exactly what they are supposed to do.

Teachers can incorporate ASL into their classroom routines in a variety of ways. You can take attendance by finger spelling the children's names while you say them. For calendar activities, children can learn to sign the days of the week and weather vocabulary. Classroom jobs such as feeding pets, helping set up snack, washing tables, or leading the line can be expressed with your voice and ASL. You can explain the daily schedule to the children in ASL, and post ASL signs for different classroom centers, such as art, blocks, books, or dramatic play.

EASE TRANSITIONS

Changing from one activity to another can often be a very hectic and chaotic time in an early childhood classroom. Sometimes very young children have difficulty stopping their play, cleaning up materials, and refocusing on new information. Sign language can help to ease these transitions by quieting down the tone of the classroom, grabbing the children's attention, and communicating directions clearly.

One of the easiest ways to begin is to flick the lights in your room as a signal for the children to stop and look at you. Use your voice and signs to give directions such as "clean up time," "sit down on the rug," "get your coats," "wash hands for snack," or "line up for recess." As with your classroom routines, you will not need to use your voice many times before you can say, "Okay, children, I'm going to sign the directions to you. See if you can guess what I'm telling you." They will enthusiastically watch you and eagerly do what you ask.

In addition, ASL is very helpful during transitions from a large group activity into small groups. You can sign colors on the children's clothing to dismiss them ("If you are wearing this color, you may go make a choice"), finger spell their names, or sign their favorite animal ("If this is your favorite animal, you may go line up"). Finger plays and songs in sign language will always grab the attention of the group, refocus wiggly kids, and fill time for impatient children.

ADDRESS DIFFERENT LEARNING STYLES

In order to effectively manage your classroom, you need to meet the needs of the diverse learners in your care. Young children have different learning styles. Some need to sit quietly and observe activities before they will join in, while others dive in with both feet and bounce from one game to the next. Some children can be read something in a book or told new information and they will understand. Others need to see it, hear it, smell it, feel it, and roll their whole body around in it before they understand. Using ASL with your students helps you address these various learning styles.

Spoken English is an auditory language—you have to use your ears to understand it. For some children, being told information is not enough for them to process. ASL is a visual language—the children see you communicating and often the

signs you will show them look like the word they stand for. ASL also uses movement—very important in young children's lives! When you and the children are signing, you are not sitting still, but rather using your bodies to express and understand language, ideas, and thoughts. For the visual and physical learners in your class, sign language is a perfect match. When you combine signing and speaking to play games, read stories, and sing songs, you can create a learning environment that addresses everyone's needs.

INCREASE COMMUNICATION WITH CHILDREN WITH SPECIAL NEEDS

You will probably have children in your care from time to time who have special needs. They may have physical or learning disabilities, special emotional needs, developmental delays, hearing issues, behavior problems, or a variety of other concerns. ASL benefits all young children in many ways, but is especially useful in helping children with certain developmental challenges.

Incorporating American Sign Language into your work with students who have language delays or difficulties can be very valuable. For example, children who have autism often have a great deal of difficulty processing spoken language. Sign language seems easier for them to understand and signs can be used as visual reminders to give directions or explain an activity. Signing with children who have language difficulties will help to increase their communication skills, both understanding and being understood. This increased communication can help avoid frustration and behavior problems, and improve interaction with other children.

Using ASL also benefits children who are "active" learners. We know most young children are active learners, but some more than others! You know, the child that is bouncing off the walls and just cannot sit still, even for a story.... Signing really helps these children focus and calm down. First of all, they are motivated to pay attention to figure out what you are doing. Second, they are thrilled to be able to use their bodies to learn and communicate. Engaging all their senses in learning helps them make connections and understand new ideas. Finally, in our experience, we have found that these "kinesthetic" learners (who can sometimes be our most challenging students) are typically the ones who learn ASL fastest and use it most often.

CREATE A COMMON LANGUAGE IN A MULTILINGUAL CLASSROOM

Today many early childhood classrooms include children whose home language is other than English. These ESL (English as a second language) students can sometimes find school to be a frustrating or frightening place, especially when their peers and teachers cannot communicate with them. While it is important that these students have access to their home language as much as possible at school, sign language can be used as a "bridge" to make connections between a child's home language and English.

Learning American Sign Language is an invaluable tool for these children to help them communicate with their classmates and teachers. The ESL students in our classrooms would sign frequently with their home language at first, and then gradually use the English word with signing. For example, a little boy from Cambodia would sign "thirsty" when he needed a drink by stroking his throat with his finger and saying "thirsty" in his native language. As the year went on he could say "thirsty" in English, and would still make the sign.

Again, because many of the signs are iconic (the hand shape or movement looks like a "picture" of the word), ASL makes a lot of sense to these children and offers them another way to communicate their needs, feelings, and ideas. When other children or teachers sign to them, it helps them focus their attention on the person communicating. In addition, ASL benefits a classroom where many languages are spoken by creating a common language and putting everyone on the same level learning to sign together.

HELP CHILDREN UNDERSTAND AND EXPRESS FEELINGS

An important part of any classroom management plan is teaching the children in your care how to appropriately deal with conflicts. One way American Sign Language can assist with this is by helping young children understand and express a variety of feelings. Some of the first signs to teach your students are vocabulary words for feelings. (See chapter 7 for complete lesson plans.) You can move beyond happy, mad, and sad and include signs for more complex emotions. The students in our classes typically know about forty signs for their emotional vocabulary, including proud, shy, bored, silly, curious, and excited.

The ASL signs for feelings can be dramatic and use a lot of facial expression. For example, to make the sign for excited, the signer makes a gleeful face with mouth open and eyes wide, while thumping her chest to indicate her heart beating wildly! The children really enjoy making these signs, and the signs help them understand the nature of the emotions. We practice and review these feeling signs all year, adding new vocabulary each time. They are the most common signs the children use in the classroom.

Learning signs for feelings gives children alternative ways to express themselves emotionally. If they are in a conflict situation, this can be of great benefit, because in place of yelling or hitting, they can use their bodies to make a dramatic sign like "furious," or "angry," or "frustrated." They get to do something physical, but not destructive. In addition, teachers often tell children to "use your words" but this can be challenging for young children, especially when they are upset. Signing their feelings is sometimes more satisfying and effective.

CALM THE CLASSROOM

Speechless communication from across the room, changing behavior without using words, and learning new, dynamic vocabulary to express feelings all contribute to creating a calm classroom environment. Using American Sign Language in an early childhood classroom does not mean that your classroom will be silent, with everyone happily expressing themselves with their hands. However, you will likely discover that after you begin to include signing in your classroom management strategies the noise in your classroom will be more like a quiet hum, with busy and productive children.

Instead of yelling across the room to tell you they want to paint, children can sign "paint, me, now?" Instead of crying if they get pushed out of line a child can sign "not friendly" or "frustrated." Instead of your shouting directions over the voices of twenty-one five-year-olds, you can begin a signing song to grab their attention, lowering your voice as you go until everyone is just signing silently.

In addition, teachers can communicate in ASL to one another in confidence or from far away without yelling. Signing can be used at times when it is inappropriate to be loud, like nap time. If the teacher is reading a story or teaching a lesson, instead of interrupting with "Can I go to the bathroom?" a child can just make eye contact and sign "toilet." A nod from the teacher is all it takes and off he goes! If you appreciate a productive, peaceful classroom without loud voices, interruptions, and conflict, sign language is a valuable tool to help you achieve this goal.

BUILD COMMUNITY

When we think about building classroom community, we think about children and adults feeling a sense of ownership of the classroom environment, communicating with each other respectfully, and learning and playing together collaboratively. Adding American Sign Language to an early childhood curriculum helps foster this sense of community for students, teachers, and families.

Children involved in programs that include ASL as a means of communication appreciate the calm tone of the classroom and will remind each other that "we do not yell in our class." They are given tools to communicate effectively with each other, regardless of their verbal language skills. This reduces frustration and conflict. In addition, the children enjoy playing the sign language games together, without the help of a teacher. Playing the

Basket Game (see p. 66), or bingo (see p. 124), or just looking through the ASL dictionary for new signs are popular choices. Children will help each other remember signs, play cooperatively with many different classmates, and stay with the sign language activities for long periods of time.

For the teachers and other staff members who begin teaching and learning ASL with hearing children, it can be a wonderful collaborative venture. You will all be learning together, hopefully, and can help one another learn new signs and ideas for including them in your curriculum. When we were learning, we would often practice signing during our lunch hour and after school. Of course, as you begin to experience the tangible benefits and desirable results of integrating signing with your program, other teachers will want to know how you do it!

Not long after you begin signing with your students, you will probably notice an increase in participation from your students' family members. This is due to the fact that your students will inevitably bring their excitement about learning ASL home to their families. Young children love learning to sign and are so proud to share their new skills and teach their parents and siblings something new. Family members are overwhelmingly enthusiastic and want to share in the learning. Many families we know have even begun using ASL at home for "family management"! Connecting your students' learning at school to their home life is one of the best ways to build a successful learning community. The addition of American Sign Language to your classroom will allow you to do this and more!

CLASSROOM MANAGEMENT SIGNS

On the following pages, you'll find signs that can be especially helpful with classroom management.

CLASSROOM MANAGEMENT SIGNS

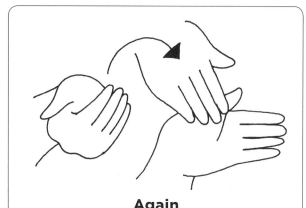

Again

With your left hand open in the "5" position and palm up, your right hand in the right-angle position, fingers pointing up, arch over, and fingers of right hand land in left palm.

Close (door)

Both hands in "B" shape held palm out, in front of your body, come together and touch.

Every Day

Place the right "A" hand on side of cheek and move it forward several times.

Don't Know

Make the sign for know, then pull hand to the right ending in the "5" hand (shows it is not in the brain).

Don't Like

Show the sign for like, then turn palm away from body and flick away ending in "5" hand fingers pointing away from the body.

Don't Want

"5" hands facing body suddenly swing around with palms down.

Cleanup

With both hands flat, one wipes off the other.

Coat

The tips of "A" hands show the lines of the front of your coat moving from collar to waist.

Come

Both index fingers make a beckoning movement.

Finish

With "5" hands facing each other, swing around simultaneously and quickly to palm-out position.

Focus

Both hands' fingers facing up and together are held at the side of your face and pulled straight out from the face.

Forget

The right-hand fingers pointing left touch the forehead and wipe knowledge from the brain while moving right and ending in the "A" position with thumb facing up.

Friendly

Have both hands in "5" position, palms facing backward, placed on either side of your face.

Get/Receive

With both hands in "5" position held in front of your body, bring in toward your chest while closing hands to "A."

Go

Both index fingers move in an arch together away from body.

Hello

The right open hand waves back and forth (also means good-bye).

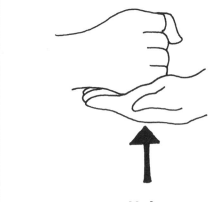

Help

With the right hand closed and resting on the left open palm, lift both hands together.

I/Me

Point to yourself using index finger.

Line Up

Place both hands in the "B" shape with fingers spread apart, left in front of right. Pull hands apart to show an imaginary line of people.

Listen

The right hand is cupped behind the right ear.

Lock

Flat left palm facing out, right "X" hand turns in palm of left hand.

No

The right index and middle fingers tap the thumb.

Noise/Noisy

Right index finger points to right ear, then both hands pull away from body in "5" hands.

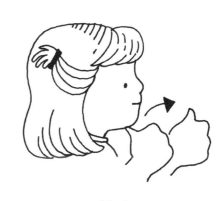

Not

The right thumb is tucked under the chin and pulled forward.

Not Yet

With the right hand in the "5" position hanging loosely and straight down your right side, move it back and forth a few times.

Please

Open right hand makes circles on chest.

Quiet/Calm/Peaceful

Both hands are open and crossed before the mouth with palms facing opposite directions. Then both hands move outward to either side at the same time.

Remember

Make the sign for know and then pull it away from forehead into the "A" hand, where it meets with your other hand in the "A" shape with thumbs touching.

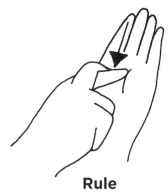

Rule

Open left hand, palm facing out, represents the piece of paper with the rules listed on it. The right hand in the "R" position strikes the middle of the left fingers, then moves down in an arc and rests against the base of the left hand.

Sit

The right index and middle fingers are draped over the same two fingers of the left hand.

Slow

Slowly pull your right hand over the back of
your left hand from fingertips to wrist.

Stand

Right hand held in upside-down "V" stands
in upturned palm of left hand.

Stop

With both hands open, the right hand with
little finger down strikes left hand.

Thank You

A flat right hand with all four fingers held
to lips moves a few inches forward.

Time

Use your right index finger, slightly curved
to tap on the back of your left wrist
(like it is your watch) several times.

Toilet

"T" hand shaking.

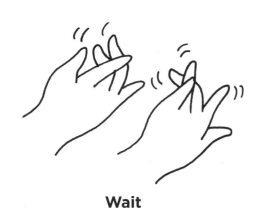

Wait

With both hands in upturned "5" position, with the right slightly behind the left, wiggle all fingers.

Wrong

Right hand in "Y" shape facing the body is brought up to touch the chin.

Yes

Make a right "S" hand and have it nod like a head.

CHAPTER 7

THEMATIC

LESSON PLANS

In this final chapter of our book, we present forty sign language lesson plans for you to use in your early childhood classroom. The lessons are organized by theme and include feelings, family, school, food, colors, seasons, community helpers, and animals. Each thematic unit contains five lesson plans complete with illustrations that show you how to sign the vocabulary, a list of children's books, and lyrics to several songs.

You should understand that the thematic lesson plans presented in this chapter do not represent a complete American Sign Language curriculum for an early childhood classroom. We recommend that you use these lesson plans in addition to including signing in your daily routines, literacy activities, and classroom management plan. These activities, along with signing vocabulary from high-quality children's books and signing interactive songs, provide simple, fun, and age-appropriate methods for sharing ASL with young children.

THE ASL ILLUSTRATIONS

The ASL illustrations in this book are arranged alphabetically and by theme. Some are located at the end of chapters—for example, you will find all the "classroom management" vocabulary signs at the end of chapter 6. Most of the sign illustrations are found in this chapter (chapter 7), organized by theme. All the illustrations include a sketch of someone forming the sign and a brief description of how to shape and move your hands. The illustration captions may include phrases like "With the 'A' hand, move down and across your chest." "A" hand means that your hand is in the shape of the sign language letter "A" while you make the sign. In addition, be sure to notice facial expressions, as they are an essential part of the language. To help you locate the illustrations in our book quickly, we have included a sign illustration index (see p. 188). The illustrations are limited to the vocabulary you will need to teach the lessons in this book. You and your students will likely want to know how to sign other words, so we recommend that you get at least one American Sign Language dictionary to use as a reference in your classroom.

We have included tips in many lesson plans about how to use ASL correctly when signing sentences, stories, and songs. Please refer to the suggestions in chapter 4 regarding teaching and learning about ASL to answer additional questions. Again, we highly recommend that you collaborate with someone who is deaf and/or proficient in ASL to learn even more about this wonderful language and how you can use it accurately and appropriately in your classroom.

UNIT ORDER

Plan to spend about a month on each unit, which will involve learning new ASL vocabulary through games, choice time activities, and signing words from songs and story books. We put the lessons in the order that we teach them throughout the school year (with the exception of the "seasons" unit), and we have found this to be an effective program. We start with feelings as the first theme, as these signs seem to be the most understandable and frequently used. Our hope is that many of these themes are common in early childhood classrooms and may overlap with activities you are already doing. This will make the integration of ASL even more simple and effective.

INTRODUCING ASL VOCABULARY

To introduce the new ASL vocabulary in each thematic unit we use the "Basket Game," which involves collecting objects or pictures that represent the words you are teaching. We've included suggestions for finding different objects to represent the vocabulary, for example, using small plastic animals for your animal basket or school supplies for your school basket. You can use your own resourcefulness to find objects or pictures to represent more obscure vocabulary, like "mountain" from the winter basket or "teacher" from the community helper basket. We have usually been able to scour our classrooms to find an object we need, and pictures work just as well. Also, the children are quite capable of stretching their imagination to accommodate less than perfect representations.

USING CHILDREN'S BOOKS

Each theme unit includes a list of children's books that you can use to reinforce the new ASL vocabulary. In addition to choosing high-quality literature that includes diverse people and situations, we have carefully chosen books that contain relevant vocabulary words. Many of the books include vocabulary from more than one unit, which allows you to build signing skills by reviewing signs while learning new ones. For example, for the animal unit, we include the book *Color Zoo* (Ehlert, 1989), which contains color vocabulary that the children will already know.

As you share these books with the children, you can sign specific words from the text as you read them, or just sign the vocabulary without using your voice. Encourage the children to "read" your signing and do the signs with you. As your vocabulary increases, you will be able to sign whole phrases and maybe even entire stories. When you do this, remember that ASL is not a word-for-word translation of English. For example, if you were sharing the book *Brown Bear, Brown Bear, What Do You See?* (Carle, 1992), in ASL it would look like "brown bear, brown bear, you see?" and you would shrug your shoulders and have a questioning expression on your face. This is an example of a situation where it's helpful to have the support of someone who is fluent in ASL and can help you with correct ASL sign choice and syntax.

SONGS

The songs we provide to accompany each unit are also to be used to reinforce the ASL vocabulary and give the children the opportunity to use the signs they are learning. Many of the songs include "audience participation" and the children get to choose which signs to use and make up new verses to suit their interests. Just as with the books, you can choose to sign only some words from a song, sing and sign at the same time, or learn to "turn your voices off" and sign an entire song. The children absolutely love to sign songs without using their voices!

A FINAL WORD

The journey of teaching and learning American Sign Language with young hearing children is worth taking. You do not need to purchase expensive classroom materials, significantly change what you are already doing, or be an expert in ASL to begin signing successfully in your classroom. We think that once you start down the path of including sign language in your work with young children, you will never turn back. We hope this book encourages you to learn the beautiful language of ASL, invented and owned by people who are deaf, and share it with your students. The rewards are many and great!

FEELINGS

Funny Face
Practice using facial expressions 54

How are You Feeling?
Introducing signs for feelings 55

Jack-in-the-Box
Review feeling vocabulary
and introduce new signs. 56

Photo Feelings
Using signs to describe feelings 57

Friendly/Not Friendly
Situational role play 58

Book List 59

Songs 59

Illustrations 60

FUNNY FACE

This is a pantomime game that a volunteer from the Deaf community shared with us. She wanted to introduce the children to acting out things with their facial expressions and body movement, with no voice. ASL uses a lot of facial expressions, especially the "feeling" signs, and is quite animated. Playing this game warms the children up to this form of communication.

GOALS

- To use facial expressions and pantomime
- To practice communicating ideas with bodies and not voice

MATERIALS

None

PROCEDURE

Have everyone sit in a circle. Say, "I have some magic chalk to share with you today. It will help us play a fun game and make silly faces." Hold up your (invisible) "chalk" and pretend to break off pieces and give one piece to each child to hold.

When everyone has a piece of "chalk," pretend to draw a line from your mouth up over your head. Pull the line up, acting as if it opens and closes your mouth. Do it slowly and then quickly. Encourage the children to mimic you. Draw a new line from your mouth to one side of your head. Pull the imaginary line in and out so that your mouth moves from side to side. Repeat, going from your chin down. Move the line quickly and slowly, making animated faces.

NOTE

The children will watch very intently and mimic the facial expressions along with the teacher. They laugh quite a bit at the silly faces!

FOLLOW-UP

This game can be a good warm-up to a sign language lesson. It gets the kids focused and ready to be expressive.

HOW ARE YOU FEELING?

Feeling signs are appropriate to introduce early in the school year. The signs are very expressive and easily understandable to the children. Learning ASL signs for emotions gives children another way to express themselves and can help ease conflict and frustration.

Begin with a children's book that has a lot of different feeling vocabulary. *How Are You Peeling: Foods with Moods* by Saxton Freymann and Joost Elffers and *Today I Feel Silly* by Jamie Lee Curtis are good books to read that lead to general discussion of different emotions.

GOALS

- To learn new vocabulary words to describe feelings
- To learn several ASL signs for feelings

MATERIALS

- Children's book with feeling vocabulary words

PROCEDURE

Read one of the above books and discuss different vocabulary words for feelings. Show the children the signs for the feeling vocabulary in the book. Demonstrate the sign and have the children sign back. Facial expression goes along with the feeling signs, so encourage children to really dramatize.

After going through the vocabulary in the book, ask children to think of a feeling they would like to see the teacher sign. Encourage creative answers beyond the typical "sad," "happy," and "mad."

NOTE

The children enjoy learning these signs and use them often. Dramatic facial expressions help the children understand the feelings.

FOLLOW-UP

This lesson can be repeated often, adding new feeling signs to increase vocabulary.

Also, remember to encourage the children to use the feeling signs throughout the day.

LESSON PLAN

JACK-IN-THE-BOX

This is a circle time game for reinforcing the sign language vocabulary for feelings. It can be played a week or so after introducing the feeling signs.

GOALS

- To review signs for feelings
- To have children practice expressive signing and make choices about what signs to use

MATERIALS

None

PROCEDURE

Gather in a circle and have the children crouch down and hide their faces. The teacher says, "Jack-in-the-box, Jack-in-the-box, feeling so (choose a feeling). Won't you come out?" The children respond, "Yes, I will" and pop up, while making the sign for the chosen feeling. Example: "Jack-in-the-box, Jack-in-the-box, feeling so sad. Won't you come out?" "Yes, I will" (pop up with a sad face and hands indicating tears coming down cheeks).

NOTE

The children like to choose which feeling sign to do and especially enjoy doing very "dramatic" signs like furious, bored, and excited. Watch to see if they make the correct sign when they pop out of the box. Notice which signs the children choose and encourage them to choose a variety of feelings.

FOLLOW-UP

You can continue to play this game all year long. The children never get tired of it and it is a great way to keep reinforcing the use of the feeling signs.

This game can also be played using other sign language vocabulary, such as animals. Example: "Lion in the box, lion in the box, so quiet and still. Won't you come out? Yes, I will." Then the children come out, doing the sign for the animal.

PHOTO FEELINGS

This activity can be done with a large or small group of children, or put out as a choice time center. It is best played after the children have had time to practice the feeling signs and are comfortable with the vocabulary.

GOALS

- To practice expressing ASL feeling signs
- To develop understanding of diverse emotions
- To practice "reading" the feelings of others

MATERIALS

- Images of diverse people expressing emotions

PROCEDURE

1. Show one of the images to the children. Ask them to tell you what they think is going on in the picture.

2. Ask them to show you a "sign" for how they think the person/people are feeling.

3. Discuss how they can tell what the person/people are feeling by looking at them and their expressions. Help them notice how the ASL sign is similar to the emotional expressions.

For example, show the children a photo of children running and smiling. Ask questions like these:

- "What is going on in this picture?"
- "What do you notice about the children's faces?"
- "Can you show me a sign that would tell me how these children are feeling?"

The children might sign "excited," "happy," "funny," or even "hot."

NOTE

Continue to discuss how children can "read" the facial expressions and body language of others to know what they are feeling. You can even go on to discuss how they might respond to some of the situations in the pictures. How could they help someone feel better? Would they feel the same way or differently?

FOLLOW-UP

This activity works well as a choice time center for small groups of children to play with a teacher or independently. You can also use these photo images to play the Basket Game with feeling vocabulary.

FRIENDLY/NOT FRIENDLY

Two signs that we use often to communicate with our students about their behavior are "friendly" and "not friendly." This role playing activity helps children understand when their actions are "friendly" and when they are not.

GOALS

- To use role play to demonstrate friendly and not friendly behavior
- To give children opportunities to practice "friendly" actions

MATERIALS

None

PROCEDURE

Tell the children that you are going to show them some different situations that might happen in the classroom and you want them to tell you if the people are being friendly or not friendly. Show them the signs for "friendly" and "not friendly."

With a child or another teacher, act out a situation like one of these (or make up your own):

A child is playing with a truck. Another child comes over and really wants to play with the truck. She grabs the truck and runs away. Friendly? Not friendly?

Then play the same situation, but have the second child ask to use the truck when her friend is finished. Friendly? Not friendly?

Two children are gluing at the art table when another child comes over to join the activity. There are only two bottles of glue, so the children say, "Go away, there is no glue for you." Friendly? Not friendly?

Then play it again with the children noticing the third child and offering to share their glue so he can join the activity. Friendly? Not friendly?

FOLLOW-UP

After giving your students a few examples, have them come up with ideas of situations that might happen in the class or outside on the playground.

Throughout the day, watch the children and sign "friendly" when you see them help a friend, share a toy, or just be kind to another child. When you see a child acting "not friendly," act surprised and catch her eye with a big smile and the "friendly" sign to remind her to change her behavior.

BOOKS ABOUT FEELINGS

Aaron, J. 1998. *When I'm afraid*. New York: Golden Books.

Aaron, J. 1998. *When I'm angry*. New York: Golden Books.

Aliki. 1986. *Feelings*. New York: Harper Trophy.

Borgman, J. 2001. *Mood swings: Show 'em how you're feeling*. Los Angeles: Price Stern Sloan.

Conlin, S. 1990. *All my feelings at preschool*. Seattle: Parenting Press.

Curtis, J. 1998. *Today I feel silly: And other moods that make my day*. New York: HarperCollins.

Freymann, S., and J. Elffers. 1999. *How are you peeling? Foods with moods*. New York: Arthur Levine.

Frost, H. 2000. *Feeling angry*. Mankato, Minn.: Capstone Press.

Hauseman, B., and S. Fellman. 1999. *A–Z Do you feel like me?* New York: Dutton Books.

Modesitt, J., and R. Spowart. 1996. *Sometimes I feel like a mouse*. New York: Scholastic.

Parr, T. 2000. *The feeling book*. New York: Little Brown.

Polland, B. 1997. *Feelings: Inside you and out loud too*. Berkeley, Calif.: Tricycle Press.

SONGS ABOUT FEELINGS

Sometimes I'm Happy
To: Farmer in the Dell

Sometimes I'm happy, sometimes I'm happy
When I feel happy I smile a smile
Sometimes I'm happy.

Sometimes I'm worried, sometimes I'm
    worried
When I'm worried my face looks down
Sometimes I'm worried.

Sometimes I'm excited, sometimes I'm excited
When I'm excited I jump up and down
Sometimes I'm excited.

Sometimes I'm tired, sometimes I'm tired
When I'm tired I do a big yawn
Sometimes I'm tired.

Notes: To add verses, let the children choose different emotions and ask them what they might do when they feel that way. Sign the feelings as you sing the song!

Let's Find a Friend
To: Farmer in the Dell

Let's find a friend,
Let's find a friend
Hi ho and cheery o
Let's find a friend!

_____ finds a friend
_____ finds a friend
Hi ho and cheery o
_____ finds a friend!

Notes: Pick a child to stand in the middle of the circle at the end of the first verse. As you sing the second verse for the first time, use that child's name in the blank. At the end of the verse, she picks a friend. Then as you sing the second verse again, the second child's name goes in the blank and he picks a friend at the end. Continue picking "friends" until all children are in the circle. You can show the ASL letter for the first letter in each child's name, and make the sign for friend, as children are chosen.

FEELING SIGNS

Bored

Right index finger touches the side of
your nostril and makes a little turn.

Brave

Both hands in "5" shape touch chest then
pull out from chest and end in fists.

Embarrassed

Both hands are placed palms facing cheeks and
move up the face to indicate a rise in color.

Excited

Both index fingers alternately strike
the heart in small circles.

Face

Right index finger draws a circle around your face.

Friendly

Have both hands in "5" position, palms facing
backward, placed on either side of your face.

Full

The down-turned right hand moves from the chest until it bumps the chin.

Funny

Right "H" hand taps end of nose.

Happy

Open right hand, palm facing body, strikes the heart in a circular motion.

Hungry

A right claw hand, palm facing chest, pulls down the chest several times.

Hurt

Both index fingers face each other and twist almost touching.

Lonely

The index finger of the right "1" hand moves straight down across your lips several times.

Mad

The right "5" hand held like a claw in front of the face strikes down or in a circle.

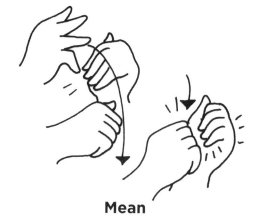

Mean

Both "A" hands are held before the chest, the right one above the left. The right hand strikes down on the left with force.

Nervous

Both "5" hands are held palms down and trembling.

Nice

The right hand slowly wipes the upturned left palm from wrist to fingertips (same as clean).

Proud

The thumb of the right "A" hand, palm down, moves up along the right side of the chest.

Sad

Both hands in "5" position, palms facing the eyes and fingers slightly bent, drop simultaneously to mouth level.

Scared

Both hands' fingers, placed side by side in front of chest, quickly open and come together trembling over the heart.

Shy

Back of the fingers on the right hand, held in the right-angle position, are placed against the right cheek and the hand moves along the cheek ending with the fingers pointing over the ear in an open hand.

Sick

The right middle finger touches the forehead and the left index finger touches the stomach. Let your tongue hang out a bit.

Silly

With the right hand in a "Y" shape, the thumb, almost touching the nose, wiggles back and forth.

Snob

Right index finger is held straight up at end of nose and the head is tilted up a bit as finger strikes up the nose to the air above.

Surprise

Both hands are held in "O" position near the eyes and suddenly flick open, and the eyes simultaneously pop open wide.

Thirsty

The right index finger strokes the throat.

Tired

Both palms face body, and with fingertips touching the chest, they fall forward into a palm-up position and the shoulders sag in a very pronounced way.

FAMILY

The Basket Game with Family Dolls
Introducing the vocabulary 66

Look What You Can Do!
Learning vocabulary for
action words and body parts. 68

Simon Signs
Gross motor activity to
practice action words 69

Mother, May I?
Gross-motor activity to practice
family and action vocabulary 70

Doll House Center
Signing center with family dolls 71

Book List 72

Songs 72

Illustrations 73

THE BASKET GAME
WITH FAMILY DOLLS

Teachers can use the Basket Game to introduce and review sign language vocabulary. The theme of the Basket Game changes throughout the year depending on what you are studying, but the way the lesson is taught remains the same.

GOALS

- To introduce new sign language vocabulary
- To review signs

MATERIALS

- A basket or plastic bin
- Small objects that represent sign vocabulary you want the children to learn

For "family" vocabulary, use small plastic or wooden dolls and animals for the people and pets. Begin with about twelve new signs. If you can, include two or three of the same object so you will have enough for each child to have a turn choosing.

VOCABULARY

- Girl
- Boy
- Man
- Family
- Mother
- Father
- Sister
- Brother
- Grandmother
- Grandfather
- Dog
- Cat
- Fish
- Horse
- Pets

PROCEDURE

Explain with your voice before you begin that this will be a "no voice" activity and that the children will need to watch you carefully to know what to do.

Have the children sit in a large circle with you. Place the basket in front of you and sign to the children to "lock their voices." Pick up an item from the basket, place it in the center of your circle, and show the children how to make the sign. Children watch and do the sign back. Introduce ten to fifteen signs in one sitting.

When all the objects are out in the circle, sign to the children one by one "you pick up (object)." Make eye contact with the child you are signing to and remind the other children to keep their voices "locked." If the child doesn't seem to know which item to pick up, she can sign "I forget." If she picks up the wrong object, sign "try again." Try giving her the sign for another object or help by mouthing the word. If she picks up the correct object, sign "good job" or "right." Each child gets a turn to pick up an object.

Once every child is holding an object from the basket, place the basket back in the middle of the circle. You will now ask the children in sign language to place their items back in the basket. Make the sign for the object, then sign "who has?" (for example, sign "Girl. Who?"). The child with that item puts it back. Continue until all items are back in the basket.

THE BASKET GAME WITH FAMILY DOLLS (cont'd)

NOTE

Watch the children to see if they understand which object to pick up. Do they need to see the sign more than once? Do they need you to mouth the word as well?

As you repeat the lesson another day, with the same signs, notice how quickly they sign back what object you are showing.

Sometimes the children crowd the circle, to get in closer. If this happens, sign "move back." Also, to get the children's attention once voices are locked, it is appropriate to bang on the floor with your hand flat. Then sign "watch me" or "look."

FOLLOW-UP

This lesson can be repeated throughout the year to introduce new vocabulary relating to your curriculum. Also, have the basket out in the classroom, so children can practice signing alone or with a friend, during language or choice time.

To make this activity into a literacy lesson, show the children the printed words for the objects in the basket as you sign them.

You can replay this activity many times to review the vocabulary and add new signs for other family members and pets.

LOOK WHAT YOU CAN DO!

This activity will teach the children signs for body parts and action words. The children will be choosing which vocabulary to use in this rhyming action game, so we have included probable sign vocabulary that you will need. If they suggest something you do not see the sign for, look it up in one of your dictionaries.

GOALS

- To learn ASL signs for body parts and action words
- To learn a rhyming action poem

MATERIALS

None

PROCEDURE

Gather the children in a circle somewhere in your classroom or outside where there is enough room for them to move around safely. Tell the children that they are going to learn a new poem about their bodies and what they can do with them. Teach them the following poem:

Body Parts

Body parts, body parts, I've got more than a few.
I've even got a few I bet you never knew.
I can touch my _____. You can do it too.
Now watch me, children. Watch what I can do.
I can touch my _____.
You can do it too!

Note: Fill in the blanks with the name of a body part. Keep repeating with different body parts and let the children suggest vocabulary. When the children make a suggestion, sing "watch Sam, children, watch what he can do." Show them the sign for the body part.

Then move on to the second verse:

With my body, look what I can do.
I can _____. You can do it too.
Now, _____, show us something you can do.

Note: In the second verse, fill in the first blank with an action word, and then fill in the second blank with a child's name. Example:

I can spin around. You can do it too.
Now, George, show us something you can do.

As the children suggest action words, show them the signs and have them do the sign and the action.

SIMON SIGNS

This is a fun circle time game for practicing signs for action words and body parts. You can add new signs for the action words before and during the game.

GOALS

- To practice expressive and receptive body part and action signs
- To watch and follow directions in a "no voice" game

MATERIALS

None

PROCEDURE

First, review the action word signs and have the children practice the signs and do the actions. Introduce some new signs and teach them to sign "Simon Signs." (Make the letter "s" and "sign.") When you are ready to begin the game, "lock" your voices. Then sign "Simon Signs" and one of the action words. The children do the action only if "Simon Signs" prefaces the direction. Unlike the traditional game, even if the children make a mistake, they continue to play.

NOTE

Watch the children to see if they do the correct action and if they follow the "Simon Signs" directions.

The children really enjoy this game and are very focused on watching the teacher for what to do next. They learn the new signs quickly and are eager to suggest other action words.

FOLLOW-UP

New action word signs can be added each time (ask the kids for ideas). Also, as the children get better at watching for directions and become more competent with the signs, they can be given a chance to be the leader of the game.

MOTHER, MAY I?

This game helps reinforce the family, body parts, and action vocabulary the children are learning. You will also need to know the ASL numbers one through five (see page 147) to play this game. It is based on the traditional childhood game, only it uses ASL instead of voice to give commands. Because it is played in ASL, the way you will communicate directions will help show the children how ASL differs from English in structure and word order.

GOALS

- To practice sign language vocabulary for family members, numbers, actions, and body parts
- To understand how ASL uses visual motions to communicate meaning and not word-for-word translation of an idea

MATERIALS

None

PROCEDURE

The teacher starts out being the "mother" and stands at one end of the classroom or outside play area. The teacher signs to the children instructions on how to move toward her. For example, "take three small steps." In ASL you would do a small motion with the sign for "walk" and the number three. The children can move only if they remember to sign "Mother, may I?" (in ASL, "please, Mom") first. If they forget, they go back to the beginning to try again. Continue giving instructions in ASL, like "jump four" or "skip five" until one child reaches the teacher. Show them the difference between the command in English and how to communicate the idea in ASL.

Example: In English, "four big jumps"; in ASL, exaggerated big motion for "jump," then sign "four."

NOTE

This is a really fun game! It is a great way to demonstrate the difference between ASL and English language. Play outside to have more space for big movements.

Watch to see if the children do the correct movements and remember to sign "Mother, may I?" before moving. Remember to include a variety of movements and indicate with signing whether they are big or small, or fast or slow motions.

FOLLOW-UP

After playing several times with the teacher being the "mother," try letting a child have a turn to sign the movements. Change the "mother" to "brother," "sister," "grandma," "grandpa," etc.

DOLL HOUSE CENTER

This is a choice time activity center that can be set up after teaching family signs. It is an activity that allows the children to practice the signs for family members that they have learned and do more sign language independently during choice time.

GOALS

- To practice "reading" and making the "family" signs
- To experience communicating with each other without using voices

MATERIALS

- Doll house or blocks
- Doll clothes
- Family dolls
- Toy pets

PROCEDURE

Set up this doll house center in a quiet corner of your room and tell the children it is a signing center. If they choose to play there, they need to "lock their voices" and use the signs they know to communicate with each other.

NOTE

It helps a great deal when a teacher is at the center, participating with the children. Without a teacher there, they need reminders to "lock their voices." The children will be quite creative in their communication if they don't know a sign. They gesture, whisper, tap, and point quite a bit. This activity involves a lot of cooperation, and the children are good at helping each other with it.

FOLLOW-UP

This center can be left as a choice time activity for several weeks, as long as the children's interest remains.

BOOKS ABOUT FAMILIES AND SELF

Angelou, M. 1994. *My painted house, my friendly chicken and me.* New York: Clarkson Potter Publishers.

Buck, N. 1999. *Hey, little baby*. New York: Harper Festival.

Bullard, L. 2002. *My body: All about me head to toe.* Minneapolis, Minn.: Picture Window Books.

Carlson, N. 2004. *My family is forever.* New York: Viking Books.

Curtis, J. 2002. *I'm gonna like me: Letting off a little self-esteem.* New York: Joanna Cotler.

Fox, M. 1990. *Shoes from grandpa*. New York: Orchard Books.

Mayer, M. 1992. *This is my family.* New York: Golden Books.

Mayer, M. 1988. *This is my house.* New York: Golden Books.

Morris, A. 2000. *Families*. New York: HarperCollins.

Strathdee, J., and J. Wallace. 1979. *The house that grew*. Wellington, N.Y.: Oxford University Press.

Wild, M. 1993. *Our granny*. Boston: Houghton Mifflin.

Woodson, J. 2001. *The other side*. New York: Putman's Sons.

SONGS ABOUT FAMILIES

With My Family
To: The Muffin Man

Tell me what you like to do
Like to do, like to do.
Tell me what you like to do,
With your family.

Note: Pick a child and let him say one of the action vocabulary signs you have learned.

Example:
Maya likes to jump around,
Jump around, jump around.
Maya likes to jump around,
With her family.

We're a Happy Family
To: I'm a Little Teapot

I love mommy, she loves me.
We love Daddy, yes indeed.
He loves us and so you see,
We're a happy family.

There They Are Together
To: The More We Get Together

There they are together, together, together.
There they are together, a happy family.
There's mommy and daddy and sister and brother.
There they are together, a happy family.

Note: Change the lyrics to reflect the families in your class.

Example:
There's grandpa and sister and baby and brother.
There's mommy and baby and big brother and kitty.

SIGNS FOR THE BASKET GAME

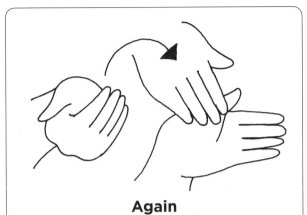

Again

With your left hand open in the "5" position and palm up, your right hand in the right-angle position, fingers pointing up, arch over, and fingers of right hand land in left palm.

Forget

The right-hand fingers pointing left touch the forehead and wipe knowledge from the brain while moving right and ending in the "A" position with thumb facing up.

Have/Has/Own(s)/Possess(es)

Fingertips of both open hands tap chest.

Lock

Flat left palm facing out, right "X" hand turns in palm of left hand.

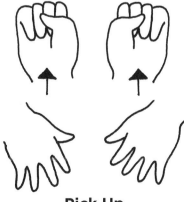

Pick Up

With both hands in open "5" position with palms down at chest level, use a grasping upward movement ending with both hands in "S" position in front of your face.

Remember

Make the sign for know and then pull it away from forehead into the "A" hand, where it meets with your other hand in the "A" shape with thumbs touching.

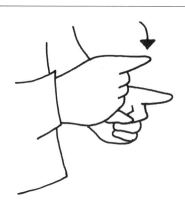

Right (accurate, correct)

The right index finger is held above the left index finger and comes down to rest on top of the left thumb joint.

Watch (verb)

A right "V" hand, palm facing your body right under your eyes, swings around and out so that fingers are now pointing forward.

Which

With both palms facing each other, move "A" hands alternately up and down in front of your chest.

Who

Thumb touches chin, and index finger bounces a bit by your mouth.

Boy/Male

Right hand palm down is held at the forehead; the fingers open and close a few times. (Baseball cap)

Brother

Right hand, palm down, is held at the forehead, fingers opening and closing a few times (boy), then with one movement point both index fingers forward and bring them together (sign for same).

Cat

Pinch your index fingers and thumbs together leaving all your other fingers standing tall (to be whiskers), then place your thumb and index fingers on either side of your nose and pinch and pull out a short distance (you can use one or both hands).

Dog

With your right hand pat your right knee and snap your fingers to call the dog.

Family

Both hands in "F" shape, palms facing away from your body, are swung out in opposite directions and circled in front until little fingers touch.

Father

Touch forehead with the thumb of your right open hand.

Fish

The open right hand, palm facing your body, swims across in front of your chest.

Girl/Female

With a right "A" hand rub thumb down the side of right cheek (girl with bonnet).

Grandfather

Place your thumb with an open hand in the middle of your forehead (father) and move hand out into small arcs.

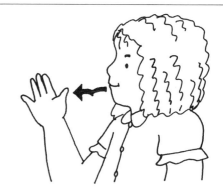

Grandmother

Place your thumb with an open hand on your chin (mother) and move hand forward in two small arcs.

Horse

Both hands in "U" form are placed on either side of your head and the index and middle fingers move forward and back (the ears of a horse).

Mother

Touch chin with the thumb of your right open hand.

FAMILY SIGNS (cont'd)

Pets

With both hands in "B" shape, brush fingertips of right hand across the back of left hand twice (like you are petting your pet).

Sister

With a right "A" hand rub thumb down the side of right cheek (girl). Then with one movement point both index fingers forward and bring them together (sign for same).

SIGNS FOR BODY PARTS / ACTIONS

Arm

Move the fingertips of your right upturned curved hand down the left arm.

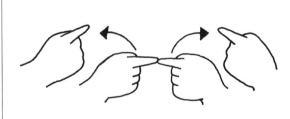

Backward

Both hands held with index fingers touching, then flip both hands backward with index fingers still extended.

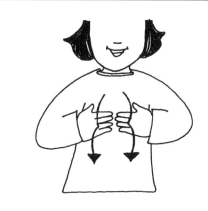

Body

Place both hands flat on your chest
and then move them lower.

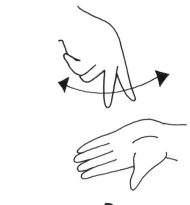

Dance

Right hand held in upside down "V" dances
in upturned palm of left hand.

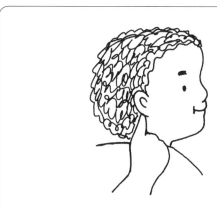

Ear

Touch your right ear.

Elbow

Tap your elbow with your index finger.

Eye

Right index finger points to your eye.

Face

Right index finger draws a circle around your face.

Fall (down)

Right hand held in upside down "V" in front of your chest arcs up and over, ending palm up.

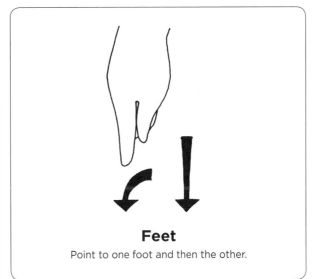

Feet

Point to one foot and then the other.

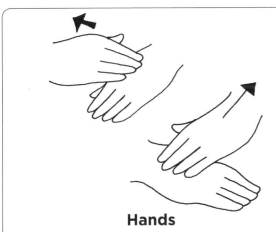

Hands

The right hand is drawn over the back of the left hand and then the left hand is drawn over the back of the right hand.

Head

Place tips of fingers at right temple and then move down in an arc and land on jaw bone.

Heart

Middle finger is placed on the heart.

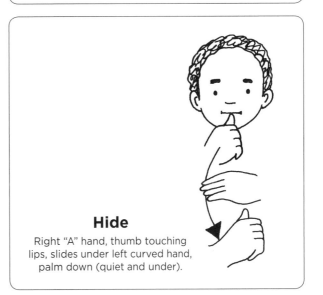

Hide

Right "A" hand, thumb touching lips, slides under left curved hand, palm down (quiet and under).

Jump

Right hand held in upside down "V" position jumps in upturned palm of left hand.

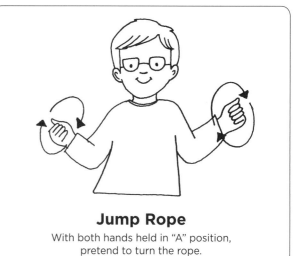

Jump Rope

With both hands held in "A" position, pretend to turn the rope.

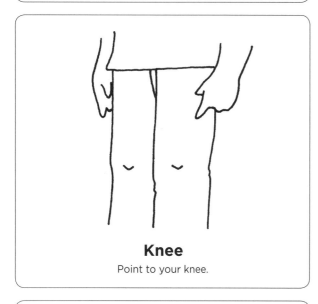

Knee

Point to your knee.

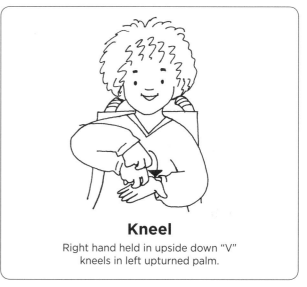

Kneel

Right hand held in upside down "V" kneels in left upturned palm.

Mouth

Point to your mouth with your right index finger.

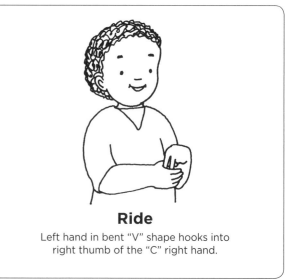

Ride

Left hand in bent "V" shape hooks into right thumb of the "C" right hand.

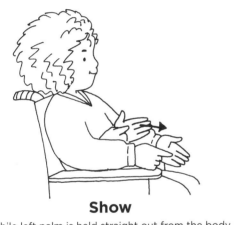

Roll

Both hands, with extended index fingers, roll over each other without touching.

Run

With two "L" hands, the right behind the left, the right index finger hooks the left thumb and the left index finger wiggles and pulls both hands forward.

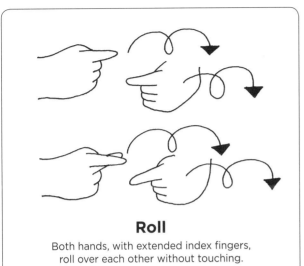

Show

While left palm is held straight out from the body, right index finger touches middle of left palm and both move straight out from your body.

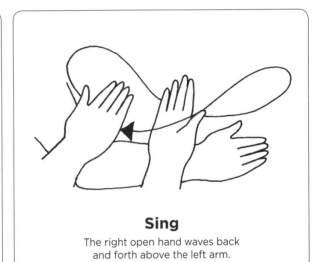

Sing

The right open hand waves back and forth above the left arm.

Sit

The right index and middle fingers are draped over the same two fingers of the left hand.

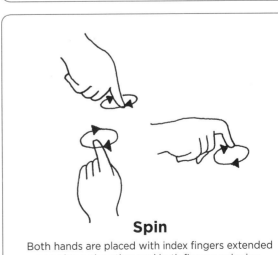

Spin

Both hands are placed with index fingers extended one above the other and both fingers spinning.

Stand
Right hand held in upside-down "V" stands in upturned palm of left hand.

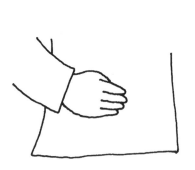

Stomach
Place one hand on your stomach.

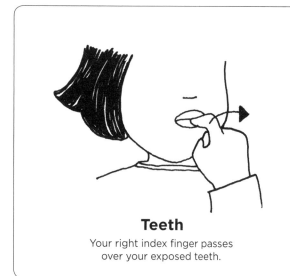

Teeth
Your right index finger passes over your exposed teeth.

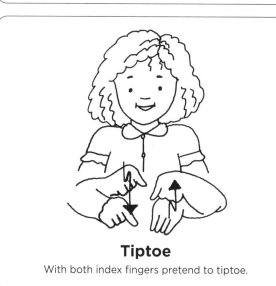

Tiptoe
With both index fingers pretend to tiptoe.

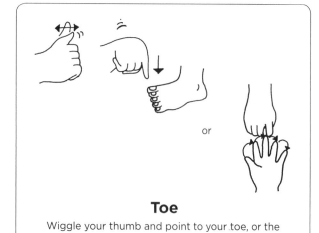

or

Toe
Wiggle your thumb and point to your toe, or the right "T" hand moves from the left thumb to the little finger indicating the toes one by one.

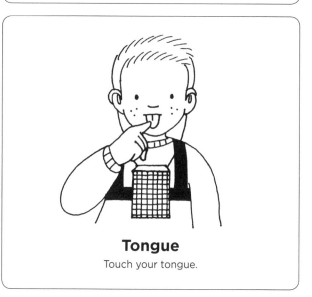

Tongue
Touch your tongue.

Walk

Use both hands in "B" shape, held in front of your chest with fingers forward, to walk like one foot and then the other.

Watch (verb)

A right "V" hand, palm facing your body right under your eyes, swings around and out so that fingers are now pointing forward.

SIGNS FOR THE DOLL HOUSE CENTER

Bathtub

Both "A" hands rub chest and then draw outline of tub with both index fingers.

Bedroom

Right cheek rests in palm of right hand, then with both hands flat, one in front of the other, palms facing body, show the four sides of the room by moving each hand to the side.

Chair

The right index and middle fingers are draped over the same two fingers of the left hand.

Door

With two "B" hands touching at thumbs with palms out, the right hand swings open from left as if it were hinged.

House

Both hands flat, palms facing each other with fingertips touching, represents the roof, then the hands pull back and down to make the walls.

Kitchen

An open right hand rests on an upturned left palm. Your right hand flips over and comes to rest with its back on the left palm (like flipping a pancake).

Picture

The right "C" hand is held in front of your face with thumb touching right cheek, then it is brought down to strike the open palm of left hand.

Refrigerator

Two "S" hands shake high on chest (sign for cold) then a box is drawn with both hands flat (cold + box).

Shower

Right hand is held with all five fingers pointing down above your head.

Sofa

The right index and middle fingers are draped over the same two fingers of the left hand. Then both hands in downturned "C" begin together and pull apart to show a couch.

Table

Right arm rests on left arm with fingers of each arm under or on top of the other elbow.

Toilet

"T" hand shaking.

Window

Both "B" hands, right on top of left with palms facing your body, pull apart like opening a window.

SCHOOL

The Basket Game
Introducing school vocabulary 88

Classroom "Go and Find"
Practice school vocabulary and
learn signs for classroom centers 90

Favorite Time Activity
Review center signs and learn
daily schedule vocabulary 91

School Center
Choice time activity center 92

Sign It!
ASL review game 93

Book List 94

Songs 94

Illustrations 95

THE BASKET GAME: SCHOOL

Use the Basket Game to introduce the "school" sign language vocabulary, just as you did to teach "family" signs. The objects you put in the basket are different, but the way the lesson is taught remains the same.

GOALS

- To introduce new sign language vocabulary
- To review signs

MATERIALS

- A basket or plastic bin
- Small objects that represent sign vocabulary you want the children to learn

For "school" vocabulary, use small items from your classroom that you want the children to know the sign for. (Check your doll house furniture for a miniature table, chair, "teacher," and "student.") If you have played the Basket Game before and have been signing with the kids for a few weeks, it is okay to introduce about fifteen new signs for the school vocabulary. Again, make sure you have enough objects in the basket for everyone to get a turn choosing. You can double up on items if you need to.

VOCABULARY

- Book
- Chair
- Crayon
- Game
- Glue
- Paint
- Paper
- Pen
- Pencil
- Puzzle
- Student
- Table
- Teacher
- Telephone

PROCEDURE

Explain with your voice before you begin that this will be a "no voice" activity and that the children will need to watch you carefully to know what to do.

Have the children sit in a large circle with you. Place the basket in front of you and sign to the children to "lock their voices." Pick up an item from the basket, place it in the center of your circle, and show the children how to make the sign. Children watch and do the sign back. Introduce ten to fifteen signs in one sitting.

When all the objects are out in the circle, sign to the children one by one "you pick up (object)." Make eye contact with the child you are signing to and remind the other children to keep their voices "locked." If the child doesn't seem to know which item to pick up, he can sign "I forget." If he picks up the wrong object, sign "try again." Try giving him the sign for another object or help by mouthing the word. If he picks up the correct object, sign "good job" or "right." Each child gets a turn to pick up an object.

Once every child is holding an object from the basket, place the basket back in the middle of the circle. You will now ask the children in sign language to place their items back in the basket. Make the sign for the object, then "who has?" (for example, sign "Pencil. Who?") The child with that item puts it back. Continue until all items are back in the basket.

THE BASKET GAME (cont'd)

Watch the children to see if they understand which object to pick up. Do they need to see the sign more than once? Do they need the teacher to mouth the word as well?

As you repeat the lesson another day, with the same signs, notice how quickly they sign back what object you are showing.

Sometimes the children crowd the circle, to get in closer. If this happens, sign "move back." Also, to get the children's attention once voices are locked, it is appropriate to bang on the floor with your hand flat. Then sign "watch me" or "look."

FOLLOW-UP

This lesson can be repeated throughout the year to introduce new vocabulary relating to your curriculum. Also, have the basket out in the classroom, so children can practice signing alone or with a friend, during language or choice time.

To make this activity into a literacy lesson, show the children the printed words for the objects in the basket as you sign them.

You can replay this activity many times to review the vocabulary and add new signs for items in your classroom or around the school. Here are some good possibilities:

- Ball
- Bus
- Coat
- Friend
- Library

- Ruler
- Slide
- Stapler
- Swing
- Toilet

CLASSROOM "GO AND FIND"

You can play this game after the children learn the sign language "school" vocabulary. The children are asked, in ASL, to go and find objects in the classroom. You can also teach the signs for different classroom centers, and include this vocabulary in the game.

GOALS

- To practice ASL school vocabulary
- To follow directions in ASL
- To learn signs for classroom centers

MATERIALS

- Objects from the Basket Game
- "Center" cards with a picture of the center activity and the printed word

PROCEDURE

Using the objects from your Basket Game, review with the children the "school" vocabulary. Just hold up each object and tell them to show you the sign. Then show them the "center" cards and how to do the signs for your classroom areas, such as the following:

- Art
- Block
- Book
- Game
- Kitchen
- Puzzle
- Science
- Writing

Tell the children this is a "no voice" game and have them "lock" their voices before you begin giving directions. Then make eye contact with and point to a child and sign "scissors, go find." She goes around the classroom, finds the object, and brings it back to the circle. If it is a center area that you asked her to find, she can just bring back something from the center. When all the children have found something, play "Put Away" by signing to each student "block, put away" or "puzzle, put away," and have them return their items to where they belong.

NOTE

This game not only reinforces the new ASL vocabulary but also helps children become familiar with their classroom, know where to find materials, and know where to put things away.

FOLLOW-UP

Use this school vocabulary throughout the day with the children and encourage them to sign to you and the other children. For example, if a child wants to paint at the easel, or wants you to read a book, you can show him how to ask in Sign. "Paint, me?" "Book, read, together?"

FAVORITE TIME ACTIVITY

This activity builds on the ASL school vocabulary and introduces signs for your daily classroom schedule. Learning signs for these often-used words and phrases will allow you and your students to use more sign language throughout your school day.

GOALS

- To review and practice school signs
- To learn signs for the daily classroom schedule
- To increase ASL use during school time

MATERIALS

- Center cards or signs from your classroom
- Daily schedule flash cards or chart

PROCEDURE

Gather the students in your circle time area and tell them that you are going to teach them more signs that they can use at school. Review the "center" signs such as blocks, books, writing, art, and science. Then look at your daily schedule chart or show them cards with the different daily activities drawn and printed on them. Ask them to help you think about the different parts of the school day, like snack time or choice time. As you talk about the different activities, show them how to sign them. The vocabulary can include signs like these:

- Story Time
- Snack
- Art
- Outside
- Circle Time
- Choice Time
- Lunch
- Library
- Reading
- Writing
- Going Home
- Signing Time

Then ask the students, in ASL, to tell you what their favorite activity is at school. Sign "favorite?" and help them sign their answers back to you.

NOTE

Learning this vocabulary will help you use sign language more often in your classroom. You can review the daily schedule and direct children to certain areas and activities without using your voice! Remember to encourage the children to use their new ASL vocabulary throughout the day. By now they know several very useful signs.

FOLLOW-UP

Turn this lesson into a math activity by graphing the answers to the "favorite activity" question. Have the children sign you their answer, and then mark on a chart or board which is their favorite time at school. Count the number of marks in each group and talk about "more" and "less."

SCHOOL CENTER

This is a choice time activity center that can be set up after teaching the school signs. It allows the children to practice the signs for the school vocabulary that they have learned and do more sign language independently during choice time.

GOALS

- To practice expressive and receptive vocabulary for the school signs
- To experience communicating with each other without using their voices

MATERIALS

- Toy school house—you can use a doll house with small figures or set up a dress-up area with "classroom" props

PROCEDURE

Set up this school center in a quiet corner of your room and tell the children it is a signing center. If they choose to play there they need to "lock their voices" and use the signs they know to communicate with each other. The children can play "teacher" and "student" and sign about what they like to do at school. They also like to pretend to "teach" the sign language lessons you have been doing with them to the other children.

NOTE

Going to this center should be a choice for the children. Some will not be comfortable enough with their expressive signing to participate but will still want to go to the center and watch. Your more competent signers will *love* this center and emerge as the leaders of the play.

It helps a great deal when a teacher is at the center, participating with the children. Without a teacher there, they need reminders to "lock their voices." The children will be quite creative in their communication if they don't know a sign. They gesture, whisper, tap, and point quite a bit. This activity involves a lot of cooperation, and the children are good at helping each other with it.

FOLLOW-UP

This center can be left as a choice time activity for several weeks, as long as the children's interest remains.

LESSON PLAN

SIGN IT!

This is a fast-moving sign language game played in teams. It is played to review ASL vocabulary. Use it only after at least a month of signing with the children, when they have had many opportunities to practice signing and know several signs.

GOALS

- To review ASL vocabulary
- To play a cooperative team game
- To practice expressive signing

MATERIALS

Flash cards with pictures of objects the children know the signs for (feeling expressions, school signs, family, body, action words, etc.). You may need to make your own by cutting out pictures and gluing them on card stock paper. In addition to the pictures, you can print the words on the flash cards.

PROCEDURE

Divide the class into two teams and have them sit across from each other in your group area. Spread the flash cards facedown on the floor between the two teams. One child from the first team chooses a card and looks at the picture. If she can do the sign, her team gets two points. If she needs help, she can sign "help" to her teammates. If they can do it then, they get one point. If no one on that team can show the sign, they have to show the card to the other team. If the other team can sign it, they get one point, and then it is their turn to pick a card. The teacher keeps score on the board.

NOTE

Keep the pace of the game fairly quick and encourage the children to help each other. Even though this sounds like a competitive game, in our experience the children are highly motivated by the team cooperation, and the score usually turns out to be a tie anyway.

FOLLOW-UP

You can use this game throughout the year to review ASL vocabulary. The children also like to play this game as a choice time activity with smaller groups.

BOOKS ABOUT SCHOOL

Baer, E., and S. Bjorhman. 1992. *This is the way we go to school*. New York: Scholastic.

Bunnett, R. 1995. *Friends at school*. Long Island City, N.Y.: Star Bright Books.

Civardi, A. 2001. *Going to school*. Tulsa, Okla.: Educational Development Corporation.

Cousins, L. 1992. *Maisy goes to school*. Cambridge, Mass.: Candlewick Press.

Crews, D. 1993. *School bus.* New York: Harper Trophy.

Edwards, B. 2002. *My first day at nursery school*. London: Bloomsbury Publishing.

Hennessy, B.G. 1992. *School days*. New York: Puffin Books.

Lillegard, D., and D. Carter. 2003. *Hello school: A classroom full of poems*. Cleveland, Ohio: Dragonfly Books.

Numeroff, L. 2002. *If you take a mouse to school.* New York: Scholastic.

Pak, S. 2003. *Sumi's first day of school ever*. New York: Viking.

Wild, M. 2000. *Tom goes to kindergarten*. Morton Grove, Ill.: Albert Whitman & Co.

SONGS ABOUT SCHOOL

Good Morning

Good morning, all you little children
With your hair just as combed as mine.
Good morning, all you little children
You're really looking fine.
Out of your pajamas and into your clothes.
Running down the road like a bunch of toads.
Good morning, all you little children
With your hair just as combed as,
Teeth just as white as,
Smile just as bright as mine!

Look Who Came to School Today
To: The Muffin Man

Look who came to school today
School today, school today.
It's my friend _____.
_____ came to school today,
School today, school today.
_____ came to school today.
_____ came to school.

Note: Insert child's name in blank.

We Like School
To: Farmer in the Dell

We like to come to school
We like to come to school
Our school is such a wonderful place
We like to come to school.

We like to play at school
We like to play at school
Our school is such a wonderful place
We like to play at school.

We like to sing at school
We like to sing at school
Our school is such a wonderful place
We like to sing at school.

Art

Your left flat hand is held in front of you and the right hand using little finger wiggles down left palm.

Ball

With both hands open, tap fingertips, making a circle.

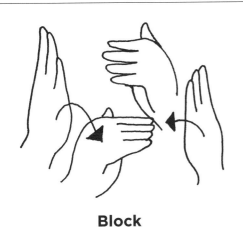

Block

Right fingertips tap left open palm above wrists, then left fingertips tap right open palm above wrist.

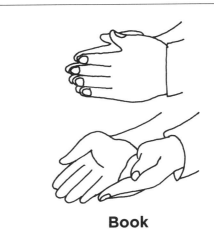

Book

Open and close both hands with little finger as the spine of the book.

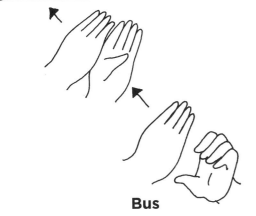

Bus

Both hands touch in "B" shape, palms facing opposite directions; then pull hands apart making left hand into a "C" shape.

Chair

The right index and middle fingers are draped over the same two fingers of the left hand.

Choice

While right hand is held in "V" shape, left hand, held in flat "F" shape, touches first index finger then middle finger of "V" hand (like pick).

Circle

Pinching your thumb and index finger together as if holding a pen, draw a circle in the air.

Coat

The tips of "A" hands show the lines of the front of your coat moving from collar to waist.

Crayon

Open "5" hand fingers touch lips (sign for color), then right hand rubs back and forth on left palm as if coloring.

Favorite

Open right "5" hand is placed with the index finger touching the chin. The hand then pivots sharply around to face out.

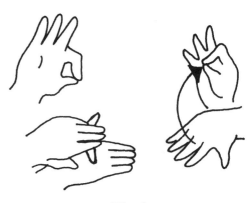

Find

Flat right hand facing palm down pinches index finger and thumb together and pulls up.

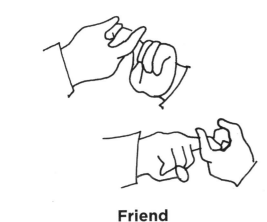

Friend

Index fingers lock, alternating left on top,
then right on top.

Game

With both hands held in "A" position, knuckles
together, thumbs wiggle facing each other.

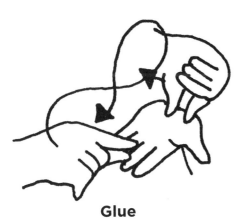

Glue

The right "G" hand is held over an open
left hand as if dripping out glue.

Go

Both index fingers move in an arch
together away from body.

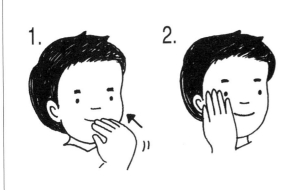

Home

With a right "O" hand place your fingers
on your lips, then move to your right cheek
(eat and sleep at home).

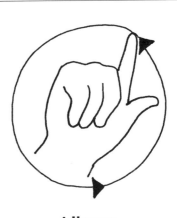

Library

A right "L" hand circles in front of your chest.

Look For

With a "C" hand, circle in front of your face as if you were searching.

Lunch

The elbow of your right arm rests on the back of your left hand (sign for noon), then your right fingers touch your mouth (sign for eat).

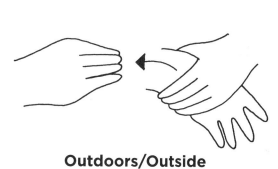

Outdoors/Outside

Your downturned open right hand, grasped loosely by your left hand, is pulled up and out of the left hand's grasp and the left hand ends in an "O" shape.

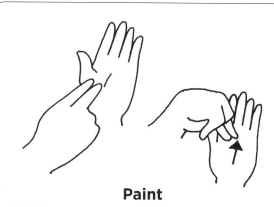

Paint

A left flat hand is held in front of your chest. The fingers of the right flat hand sweep up and down the left hand. Sometimes only the middle and index fingers are used.

Paper

With your right "5" hand, held palm toward your chest, strike your left palm hand twice. The left palm is held with fingers pointing right.

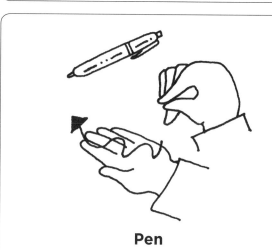

Pen

Tip of middle finger of "P" right hand writes on left palm.

Pencil

Thumb and index finger come to the mouth, as if you were going to lick the lead, then write on left palm.

Play

Both hands held in "Y" shape lightly twist back and forth simultaneously.

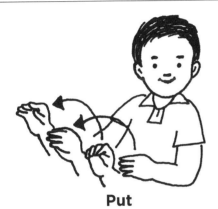

Put

Both hands in flat "O" position with palms down move one arch forward together.

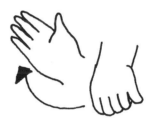

Away

With a right "A" hand facing down, move hand away from body and to the right ending in an open hand palm facing forward and down.

Read

Hold a right "V" hand in front of the left palm as if the left palm were a book and your "V" the eyes reading.

Ruler

Both hands are held in the "R" shape with thumbs touching.

School

With both hands flat, the right hand strikes the left palm twice going straight up and down (old sign comes from teacher clapping hands together to call the class in for school to begin).

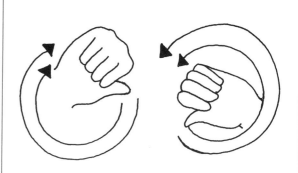

Science

Both hands in "A" shape make a circle in front of chest.

Sign

Two "D" hands circling in front of you.

Sing

The right open hand waves back and forth above the left arm.

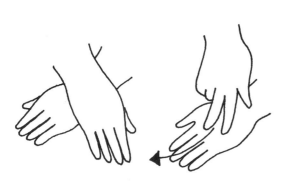

Slide

Right flat hand slides down the back of left flat hand (you can use just the index and middle fingers to represent the legs of a person sliding down).

Stapler

Both hands in "S" shape, knuckles touching, rock forward to close like a stapler.

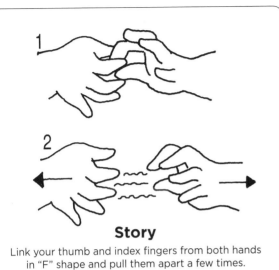

Story

Link your thumb and index fingers from both hands in "F" shape and pull them apart a few times.

Student

The downturned fingers of the right hand are placed in the left palm, then the right fingers close (as if they picked something up) and rise to the forehead. Then both hands go down the sides of the body to show "person."

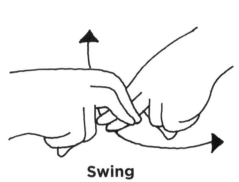

Swing

Two "U" hands are held before your chest with the right index and middle fingers crossing over the left index and middle fingers (sign for sit) and move in a swinging motion.

Table

Right arm rests on left arm with fingers of each arm under or on top of the other elbow.

Teacher

Fingertips of both hands are placed on the temples, then they swing out and open into "5" hands and move down the sides of your body.

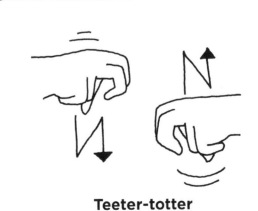

Teeter-totter

Both hands in "N" shape, held facing each other, go up and down like a teeter-totter.

Telephone

The right hand is in the "Y" shape with the thumb held near the ear and the little finger by the mouth.

Time

Use your right index finger, slightly curved to tap on the back of your left wrist (like it is your watch) several times.

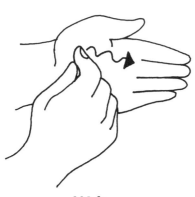

Write

Right hand holds thumb and index finger pinched together as if grasping a pen and writes on left open palm.

FOOD

The Basket Game
Introduce food vocabulary. 104

Picnic Basket
Review food vocabulary,
introduce new food signs. 105

Pass the Food
Practice food signs. 106

Restaurant
Choice time play activity 107

Snack Signs
ASL vocabulary for snack time 108

Book List 109

Songs 109

Illustrations 110

THE BASKET GAME: FOOD

Teachers can use this Basket Game to introduce and review sign language vocabulary. The theme of the Basket Game changes throughout the year depending on what you are studying, but the way the lesson is taught remains the same.

GOALS

- To introduce new sign language vocabulary for food
- To review signs

MATERIALS

- A basket or plastic bin
- Small objects that represent sign vocabulary you want the children to learn

For food vocabulary, use pretend food items from your housekeeping area for this game.

Begin with about twelve new signs. If you can, include two or three of the same object so you will have enough for each child to have a turn choosing.

VOCABULARY

- Noodles
- Corn
- Cake
- Banana
- Cheese
- Tortilla
- Apple
- Lettuce
- Popcorn
- Cookie
- Bread
- Carrot

PROCEDURE

Explain with your voice before you begin that this will be a "no voice" activity and that the children will need to watch you carefully to know what to do.

Have the children sit in a large circle with you. Place the basket in front of you and sign to the children to "lock their voices." Pick up an item from the basket, place it in the center of your circle, and show the children how to make the sign. Children watch and do the sign back. Introduce ten to fifteen signs in one sitting.

When all the objects are out in the circle, sign to the children one by one "you pick up (object)." Make eye contact with the child you are signing to and remind the other children to keep their voices "locked." If the child doesn't seem to know which item to pick up, she can sign "I forget." If she picks up the wrong object, sign "try again." Try giving her the sign for another object or help by mouthing the word. If she picks up the correct object, sign "good job" or "right." Each child gets a turn to pick up an object.

Once every child is holding an object from the basket, place the basket back in the middle of the circle. You will now ask the children in sign language to place their items back in the basket. Make the sign for the object, then for "who has?" (for example, "Cheese. Who?"). The child with that item puts it back. Continue until all items are back in the basket.

PICNIC BASKET

This is a sign language game that gives the children opportunities to show the food signs they have learned. Play this game after you have played the Basket Game with pretend food several times and feel that the children have an understanding of the vocabulary.

GOALS

- To have children practice expressive ASL—they make the signs for others to understand
- To review sign language food vocabulary

MATERIALS

- Picnic basket
- Pretend food

PROCEDURE

Sitting in a circle with the whole group or a small group of children, say, "I have a picnic basket that I want to share with you all." Hold the basket in front of you and explain that in your picnic basket there is a lot of food. Reach into the basket and pull something out. Sign what you find! Ask the children to "show you the sign" too. Then pass the basket around so each child can have a turn pulling something out and showing the sign to everyone.

NOTE

Notice if the children are using sign language to guess and if they are doing the signs correctly.

If a child does not want a turn, he needs only to "pass the basket" to the next person.

FOLLOW-UP

This game can be played again and again. Use this game to add signs like these to your food vocabulary:

- Eggs
- Chicken
- Ice cream
- Juice
- Rice
- Potato
- Pear
- Soup
- Watermelon
- Fish

Leave the picnic basket out so the children can play the game in small groups independently or with a teacher during choice or language time.

PASS THE FOOD

This is another sign language circle time game where the children practice using the food signs they learned and are introduced to new ASL vocabulary.

GOALS

- To review ASL food sign vocabulary
- To learn new food signs
- To practice "receptive" signing—understanding what someone is signing to them
- To practice "expressive" signing—making the signs for someone else to understand

MATERIALS

- Pretend food from your housekeeping center

PROCEDURE

Introduce each food by signing the name as you would for the Basket Game. Tell the children to show you the sign as you hold up the food. Give each child an item to hold. Then say, "We are going to pass food to each other. Watch me to see what to do." Then point to a child and sign "trade?" Then sign the food you are holding and the food he is holding. For example, "trade, watermelon, banana?" Pass the pretend food to each other. Then it is that child's turn to sign to someone else to pass her food. He points and looks at another student and signs "trade, milk, pizza?" Continue until every child has had a turn to practice signing to a friend!

NOTE

Help the children form signs with their hands when needed. Give a lot of support during this activity, as the children will find expressive signing more difficult.

FOLLOW-UP

This lesson can be repeated often and played with other themes to help increase sign language interaction between students.

RESTAURANT

LESSON PLAN

This is a choice time activity center that can be set up after teaching food signs. It is an activity that allows the children to practice the signs for food that they have learned and do more sign language independently during choice time.

GOALS

- To practice food sign vocabulary—expressive and receptive
- To have children communicate with each other without using their voices and without the help of a teacher
- To have children play cooperatively at this center and help each other communicate in only sign language

MATERIALS

- Table with two chairs
- Plates
- Play food
- Cups
- Aprons
- Chef hats

PROCEDURE

Two children wear aprons and hats and act as the "chefs," sitting in chairs behind the table. "Customers" approach and order their food using sign language only. The chefs prepare what they ask for and give them the pretend food.

NOTE

This choice time activity is a great opportunity to assess the children's signing abilities. First of all, notice which children choose the activity and want to play in the center at length. Watch carefully to see which signs the children use and how much they are able to communicate with no voice.

This is a very popular choice time activity. The difference in the children's signing abilities is highlighted by this activity. The more competent signers will choose to be the chefs and stay at the center for a long time. Some children come over and just watch; others understand the signs, but do not sign back. It helps a great deal when a teacher is at the center, participating with the children. Without a teacher there, they need reminders to "lock their voices." The children will be quite creative in their communication if they don't know a sign. They gesture, whisper, tap, and point quite a bit. This activity involves a lot of cooperation, and the children are good at helping each other.

FOLLOW-UP

This center can be left as a choice time activity for several weeks, as long as the children's interest remains.

SNACK SIGNS

Use this activity with real food while you are sitting with the children during snack or lunch, or practice with pretend food at circle time.

GOALS

- To review ASL food signs
- To increase sign language conversation
- To learn ASL words and phrases for table manners

MATERIALS

- Snack
- Plates
- Cups

PROCEDURE

Explain with your voice that you all will be learning sign language words and phrases to use at snack/lunch time. Introduce the new vocabulary with your voice while you show the sign. Encourage the children to make the signs with you. Show them these signs:

- Cup
- Please
- Thank you
- More
- Finished
- I like it
- I don't like it

Include signs for the food they are eating. Use your ASL dictionary to look up new food signs. Model using this new vocabulary as you eat snack or lunch with the children. Use a lot of facial expression, and mouth the words while signing at first.

FOLLOW-UP

Encourage the use of the "manners" signs throughout the day by modeling and responding to the children using the signs. As you practice more signing at snack time, try doing a five-minute "sign time." Tell the children to "lock their voices" and see how much you all can communicate just using ASL.

BOOKS ABOUT FOOD

Asplind-Riley, L. 1997. *Mouse mess.* New York: Scholastic.

Carle, E. 1969. *The very hungry caterpillar.* New York: HarperCollins.

Caseley, J. 1990. *Grandpa's garden lunch.* New York: Green Willow Books.

Ehlert, L. 1996. *Eating the alphabet.* New York: Red Wagon Books.

Fleming, D. 1996. *Lunch.* Austin, Tex.: Holt Publishing.

Hayes, S. 1993. *Eat up Gemma.* Orlando, Fla.: Harcourt.

Hoberman, M. 2000. *The seven silly eaters.* London: Voyager Books.

Howard, J. 1992. *When I'm hungry.* New York: Penguin.

Leburn, C. 1996. *Little brown bear does not want to eat.* New York: Scholastic.

Sharmat, M. 1984. *Gregory the terrible eater.* New York: Simon & Schuster.

Sharratt, N. 2000. *Ketchup on your cornflakes?* New York: Scholastic.

SONGS ABOUT FOOD

I Love Food

I love food. Yes, I love food.
I love carrots and broccoli and ice cream.
I love milk and oranges and peanuts.
My tummy is hungry, and I want some food.
I love it because it's food.

Note: Let the children choose different foods to add new verses. Use the sign language food vocabulary.

Good Food
To: Old MacDonald Had a Farm

Let's all share some yummy food,
Food that's good for us.
Let's all share some yummy food,
Food that's good for us.
There are some carrots here and some
    oranges there.
Here's some lettuce, there's some broccoli.
Let's all share some yummy food,
Food that's good for us.

Oh, Do You Eat Your Vegetables?
To: The Muffin Man

Oh, do you eat your vegetables, vegetables,
    vegetables?
Oh, do you eat your vegetables, each and
    every day?

Oh, yes, we eat our vegetables, vegetables,
    vegetables.
Oh, yes, we eat our vegetables, each and
    every day.

Note: Give children a turn to pick a vegetable, then use their name and vegetable choice to continue the song.

Example:
Oh, Sam eats tomatoes, tomatoes, tomatoes.
Oh, yes, Sam eats tomatoes, each and every day.

Apple

Right "X" hand twists in right cheek.

Banana

The left index finger is held straight up (represents the banana) and the right-hand fingers go around the index finger pulling the peel off.

Beans

Right-hand tips of all four fingers move simultaneously, making little hops from the knuckle to the tip of the left index finger representing the beans in a pod.

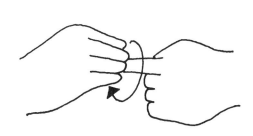

Berry

Right fingers in a loose "O" hand cover the tip of left index finger and left wrist rotates.

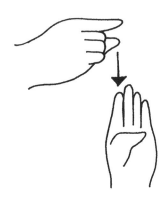

Broccoli

The left hand is held in "B" shape and the right hand, in "G" shape, taps on fingertips of left hand.

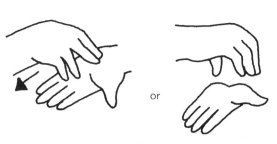

or

Cake

The fingertips of a right "5" hand are placed in the palm of the left hand and pulled first straight out left fingers then across palm (like cutting a piece of cake).

Candy

Index finger touches side of face by molar teeth and twists (like a cavity is there).

Carrot

The left index finger (the carrot) is held pointing away from your body and the right "S" hand rubs thumb and index side of fist next to left index finger as if peeling the carrot.

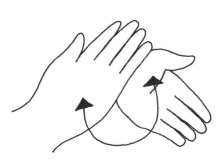

Cheese

The base of the down-turned right hand is pressed against the base of the left turned-up hand and the two pivot back and forth.

Chicken

With your right index finger and thumb pointing forward, open and close at your lips, then your right index finger in "X" shape scratches at the middle of your left palm (like pecking for food).

Cookie

Right claw hand turns in left flat palm like cutting out a cookie.

Corn

The right index finger is held across the front of lower lip and turned as if eating corn off the cob.

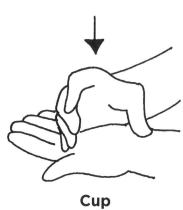

Cup

A right "C" hand is held, little finger down, onto a flat left palm.

Don't Like

Show the sign for like, then turn palm away from body and flick away ending in "5" hand fingers pointing away from the body.

Don't Want

"5" hands facing body suddenly swing around with palms down.

Eat

"O" hand, palm down, taps on lips.

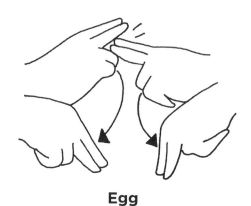

Egg

With both hands in "H," bring the right down on the left so that both hands now point down and are held slightly apart (like breaking an egg).

Fish

The open right hand, palm facing your body, swims across in front of your chest.

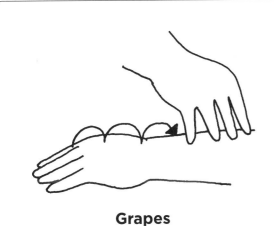

Grapes

A right claw hand moves up the back of left hand and arm in little arches (like bunches of grapes).

Hamburger

Cup both hands together alternating right on top, then left on top, like making patties.

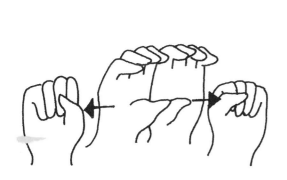

Hot Dog

Both hands in "C" shape are held side by side with palms out, thumb and index fingers touching. They move apart into "S" hands.

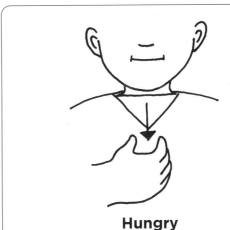

Hungry

A right claw hand, palm facing chest, pulls down the chest several times.

Ice Cream

Closed right "S" hand comes to mouth and strokes down several times as if licking an ice cream cone.

Juice

The "C" hand is tipped to your lips and then pulled away into a "J" hand.

Lettuce

Palm of an open right hand taps the side
of your head (head of lettuce).

Like

Place the thumb and index fingers of the right hand
a few inches apart in the middle of your chest, then
move the hand straight out from the chest and bring
the two fingers together simultaneously.

Lunch

The elbow of your right arm rests on the back
of your left hand (sign for noon), then your right
fingers touch your mouth (sign for eat).

Meat

With your right thumb and index finger,
grab the flesh between thumb and index
finger of left hand (beef, flesh).

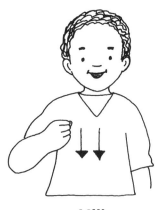

Milk

Open hand grabs and pulls down, repeating
action several times, like milking a cow.

More

Both hands are held with fingers together and palms
facing each other, then fingertips tap together.

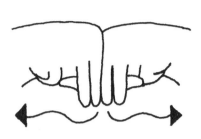

Noodle

Both hands in "N" shape pull apart and wiggle simultaneously. Sometimes the little finger is used for spaghetti noodle.

Orange

The right "C" hand is held at your mouth opening and closing deliberately as if squeezing an orange.

Pea

Right "X" hand makes little hops from left hand up left index finger, representing the peas in a pod.

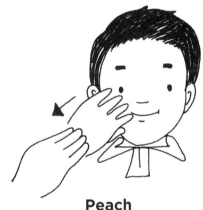

Peach

The fingers of your right hand stroke your right cheek and close into an "O" hand (the soft skin of the peach).

Peanut Butter

Scrape the back of your right thumb against the underside of your front teeth, then right hand in "U" shape swipes left open palm (like spreading peanut butter).

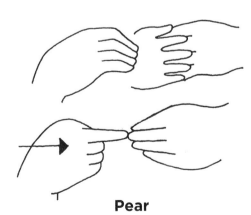

Pear

With left hand held in flat "O," right hand covers left and pulls to the right ending with index finger of right hand touching left fingers (represents the stem of the pear).

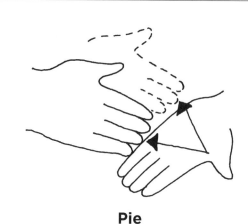

Pie

With both hands flat, use your right hand to cut a triangle (piece of pie) on the palm of your left hand.

Pizza

The right "P" hand draws a Z in the air.

Please

Open right hand makes circles on chest.

Popcorn

The index fingers from both hands alternately flick up.

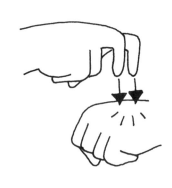

Potato

With the left hand in a fist, the right "V" hand upside down pokes the top of left hand (like poking the potato).

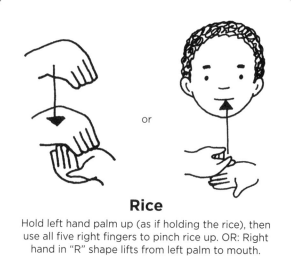

or

Rice

Hold left hand palm up (as if holding the rice), then use all five right fingers to pinch rice up. OR: Right hand in "R" shape lifts from left palm to mouth.

Sandwich

Both hands are held palms flat together and turned so that fingertips face mouth.

Snack

Pinch your right index finger and thumb together, then move to your mouth (a bit of food).

Soup

The upturned left hand represents the bowl of soup and the "H" right hand acts as the spoon lifting the soup from the hand to the mouth.

Sugar

The fingertips of the right hand, palm facing your body, brush against your chin a few times from the lips down.

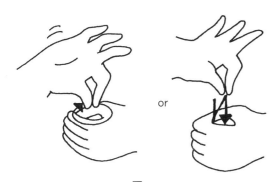

or

Tea

The right index finger and thumb raise and lower an imaginary tea bag into the left "C" or "O" hand.

Thank You

A flat right hand with all four fingers held to lips moves a few inches forward.

Thirsty

The right index finger strokes the throat.

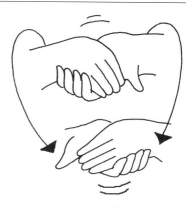

Tortilla

Both hands open cup together alternating right on top, the left on top like making tortillas (sometimes the sign for corn is made first).

Trade

Position the right "A" hand above the left "A" hand, then swing right hand down and under the left, coming up a few inches in front of left hand.

Water

With your right hand in "W" shape tap your index finger on your lip (water).

Watermelon

With your right hand in "W" shape tap your index finger on your lip (water), then with your left hand in "S" shape, take the middle finger of your right hand and flick the back of your left hand like you are knocking away the seeds.

COLORS

Color Blocks
Introducing color signs 120

Color Ball
Fast-moving circle game
to review color signs 121

I Spy
Practice color vocabulary
and review school signs .122

Who Has the Color?
Large-group game to practice
expressive signing 123

Color and Shape Bingo
Small-group board game
with color and shape signs. 124

Book List 125

Songs 125

Illustrations 126

COLOR BLOCKS

Color vocabulary is used often in an early childhood classroom. This sign language game teaches the ASL signs for colors, including the words "light" and "dark."

GOALS

- To learn to recognize colors, including dark and light
- To learn the signs for several different colors

MATERIALS

- Colored blocks

PROCEDURE

In a large-group circle time or with a small group of children, show the children some colored blocks. Show them the individual colors and how to make the sign for each color. Have them make the signs with you. Then place the colored blocks in the middle of the circle. Play the "pick up" game, where you sign to each child to pick up a certain color block. Try to include as many colors as you can and show them light and dark colors too. Once everyone has a block, sign back to them "red, who has?" or "light blue, who has?" for each child to put back her color.

NOTE

Watch the children to see if they understand which color object to pick up. Do they need to see the sign more than once? Do they need the teacher to mouth the word as well?

As you repeat the lesson another day, with the same signs, notice how quickly they sign back what color you are showing.

FOLLOW-UP

Keep the color blocks out in the classroom so children can practice signing alone or with a friend during language or choice time.

To make this activity into a literacy lesson, show the children the printed words for the colors as you hold up the blocks and sign the color name.

Use ASL in your art area! As the children use materials, encourage them to sign the colors of their markers, crayons, and paper. Have them ask each other in Sign for certain colors.

COLOR BALL

This fast-moving circle time game is a fun way for the children to practice color sign language vocabulary.

GOALS

- To review color signs

MATERIALS

- A large ball with colored sections

PROCEDURE

Have the children sit on the floor in a circle. Show them a multicolored ball—the type that has "wedges" of color. Look at all the different colors and review the color signs for each one. Explain that you will be rolling the ball to them and when the ball reaches them, they need to stop it with their hand. Then they need to look at the color their hand is on, make the sign, and quickly roll it to another child. That child does the same.

NOTE

We tell the children that the ball is like a "hot potato" to encourage them to make their sign and roll the ball right away.

FOLLOW-UP

This is a good "filler" game when you have some extra time and need a quick and fun activity.

To make it more challenging and include alphabet signs, you can ask the children to sign the first letter of the child's name that they are passing the ball to.

I SPY

This is a traditional children's game that is easily played in sign language. It reinforces color and object vocabulary signs and teaches more sign language phrases.

GOALS

- To review color and object vocabulary
- To learn new ASL vocabulary
- To increase expressive signing by the children

MATERIALS

No special materials are needed. This game uses objects found in the classroom, or wherever it is played.

PROCEDURE

In a large or small group, sit together in a circle. Begin by placing objects in the center of the circle that the children know the signs for. The teacher then "spies" something from this group of objects for the children to guess. Sign a color, and then sign "I see." The children guess in ASL what you "spy." Sign "right" or "wrong" to the guesses. Example: Teacher: "Red, I see." Children: "Apple?" "Ball?" "Scissors?" Play the game with the chosen objects first and let the children take turns being the one who "spies."

FOLLOW-UP

As the children get better at this game and their ASL vocabulary has grown, leave out the chosen objects on the floor and just let them look around the room to choose something to spy. They may need adult help choosing appropriate objects to "spy," and sometimes they give away the answer easily by looking right at it! They also have to remember to choose only objects that they and the other children know the signs for. Encourage every child to have a turn being the "spy."

WHO HAS THE COLOR?

If you have been following the lesson plans in this book in order, you are now more than halfway through, and your ASL vocabulary is quite large! You and the children are probably ready to use more conversational ASL. To encourage this in the classroom, it helps to teach the children how to form short sign language sentences. Making sentences in sign language also illustrates ASL sentence structure, which is different from English.

GOALS

- To be able to understand and make short sentences in ASL
- To practice correct ASL sentence structure
- To learn ASL vocabulary for clothes
- To practice ASL color vocabulary
- To practice the manual alphabet

MATERIALS

None

PROCEDURE

With the children gathered in a circle, review the signs for colors. Tell them to look around at what everyone is wearing and see if they can find the colors that you sign to them. Sign "blue, who has?" This game is a "lock your voice" game, so they must answer in ASL by pointing to the child or making the finger sign for the first letter in the name of a child who is wearing that color.

After doing this a few times, start adding the signs for clothes. For example, sign "blue pants, who has?" Point out the difference in ASL sentence structure to the children.

Next, you can help the children answer a question in ASL. For example, you sign "Karen, what color socks?" and the child signs back "my socks red."

NOTE

The children really need to learn the colors with concrete objects first, before you can move on to this game.

The first time you play this, the children will need help understanding the question and signing back the answer.

FOLLOW-UP

This game can be played to review new sign vocabulary and increase conversational ASL.

Give the children turns to be the signer and choose what color to look for. Encourage the children to sign back longer phrases instead of just pointing to the child with the right color. For example, you can sign "dark blue pants, who has?" and they would respond, "Sam, dark blue pants."

COLOR AND SHAPE BINGO

To reinforce vocabulary and encourage more conversational sign language, try playing the familiar children's game of "bingo" in ASL. Bingo games can introduce new sign language vocabulary, help children review familiar signs, and help with letter and sight word recognition.

GOALS

- To play a familiar game using only sign language to communicate
- To review sign language vocabulary for colors and learn shape signs
- To encourage more conversational ASL
- To learn some Deaf culturally appropriate mannerisms. For example, instead of shouting "bingo" the children bang on the table or wave their hands in the air.

MATERIALS

- Color and shape bingo game with bingo cards, object cards, and markers. This type of game can be found at any educational toy store, or you can easily make your own.

PROCEDURE

This game works best when played with a small group of children (four to six) and a teacher. Give each child a bingo card and bingo markers. First explain to the children how to play bingo if they don't already know how. Then tell them that you are going to play the game with your voices "locked." Hold up a color/shape card and tell them to show the sign. For example, sign "triangle, yellow." You can also sign "who has?" Have the kids do the sign with you. When a child fills his card and has bingo, he should wave his hands in the air, stomp his feet, or bang on the table to show he has won.

NOTE

The children especially like banging on the table when they have bingo! Many of them enjoy being the bingo "caller."

FOLLOW-UP

Let the children take turns being the bingo "caller." This is a great way for the children to practice expressive signing. You can also make custom bingo cards to play this game with other vocabulary themes.

BOOKS ABOUT COLORS

Adoff, A. 2002. *Black is brown is tan*. New York: Amistad Books.

Baker, A. 1999. *White rabbit's color book*. New York: Kingfisher.

Ehlert, L. 1989. *Color zoo*. New York: HarperCollins.

Ehlert, L. 1992. *Planting a rainbow*. New York: Voyager Books.

Hoban, T. 1987. *Is it red? Is it yellow? Is it blue?* New York: Harper Trophy.

Lionni, L. 1997. *A color of his own.* New York: Dragonfly Books.

Lionni, L. 1995. *Little blue and little yellow*. New York: Harper Trophy.

Martin, B. 1992. *Brown bear, brown bear, what do you see?* New York: Henry Holt & Co.

McMillan, B. 1988. *Growing colors*. New York: HarperCollins.

Newton-Chocolate, D. 1997. *Kente colors*. New York: Walker & Co.

Thong, R., and G. Lin. 2001. *Red is a dragon*. San Francisco: Chronicle Books.

Walsh, E. 1995. *Mouse paint*. New York: Voyager Books.

Wise-Brown, M. 2000. *Color kittens*. New York: Random House.

SONGS ABOUT COLORS

Colors
To: Twinkle, Twinkle, Little Star

Red is a flower, blue is the sea.
Purple is a gum drop and yellow is a bee.
Green like the grass and white like the moon,
Black is the night and silver is a spoon.
Orange is the sun and pink is a rose.
Are there other colors that you know?

Find the Color
To: The Muffin Man

Oh, can you find the color_____
The color _____, the color _____.
Can you find the color _____,
Somewhere in this room?

Color Clothes Game
To: If You're Happy and You Know It

If you are wearing blue, jump right up.
If you are wearing blue, jump right up.
If you are wearing blue, if you are wearing
   blue.
If you are wearing blue, jump right up.

If there is red on your shirt, hop in place.
If there is red on your shirt, hop in place.
If there is red on your shirt, if there is red on
   your shirt,
If there is red on your shirt, hop in place.

Note: Change the color, clothes, and action for new verses.

SIGNS FOR COLORS

Black

The right index finger draws a
line across your forehead.

Blue

The "B" hand shaking.

Brown

The "B" hand slides down the side
of your right cheek.

Dark

Both open hands are held in front of your face,
then they move toward each other in a slight
downward arch and cross (shutting out the light).

Green

The "G" hand shaking.

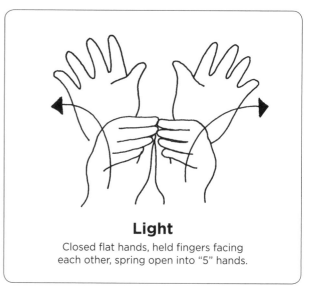

Light

Closed flat hands, held fingers facing
each other, spring open into "5" hands.

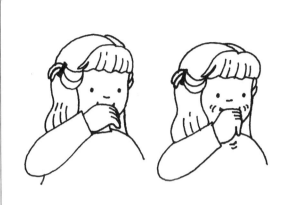

Orange
The right "C" hand is held at your mouth opening and closing deliberately as if squeezing an orange.

Purple
The "P" hand shaking.

Red
The right index finger strokes the lips.

White
An open "5" hand on your chest pulls out and closes to "O" hand.

Yellow
The "Y" hand shaking.

SIGNS FOR I SPY

I/Me

Point to yourself using index finger.

See

The right "V" hand, palm facing your body, is placed so that the fingers are just under your eyes. The hand is then pulled out a bit.

SIGNS FOR WHO HAS THE COLOR?

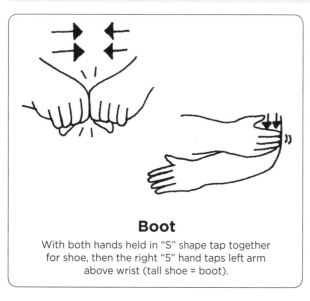

Boot

With both hands held in "S" shape tap together for shoe, then the right "5" hand taps left arm above wrist (tall shoe = boot).

Coat

The tips of "A" hands show the lines of the front of your coat moving from collar to waist.

Glasses

Both hands held in "G" shape tap the sides of your face, representing glasses.

Glove

The right hand brushes up the back of left hand from fingertips to wrist, and then left does same to right (like pulling on gloves).

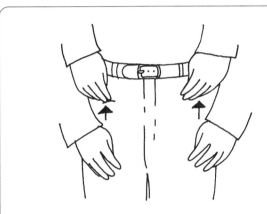

Pants

With both hands open, pull hands up from knees to thighs.

Shirt

Both hands open on your chest move down simultaneously. The action is then repeated.

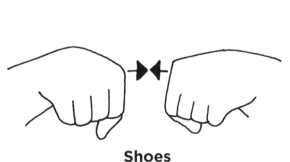

Shoes

Both hands held in "S" shape tap together in front of your chest.

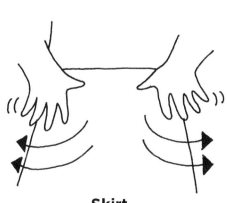

Skirt

With both hands open, hold your thumbs on your waist and wave your other fingers below.

Think

The index finger of your right hand makes
a small circle on your forehead.

What

Right index finger crosses over
left flat-hand fingers.

When

Both hands are in "D" shape. Left hand is still with
palm facing body while right hand circles left hand in a
clockwise motion and stops to meet left index finger.

Where

Right "D" hand, with index finger straight
and palm out, moves back and forth slightly.

Who

Thumb touches chin, and index finger
bounces a bit by your mouth.

Why

Place a "5" hand on side of forehead
and pull away into a "Y" hand.

SIGNS FOR COLOR/SHAPE BINGO

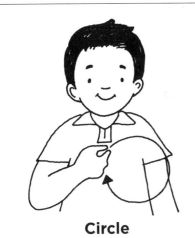

Circle

Pinching your thumb and index finger together
as if holding a pen, draw a circle in the air.

Rectangle

With both hands in "R," draw the outline
of a rectangle in the air at chest height.

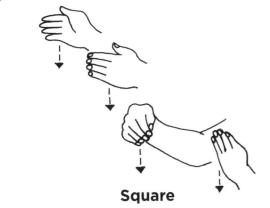

Square

With both hands open, palms facing each other, and
fingers pointing out, drop both hands simultaneously,
then shift their positions so that both palms face your
body (making a box or square).

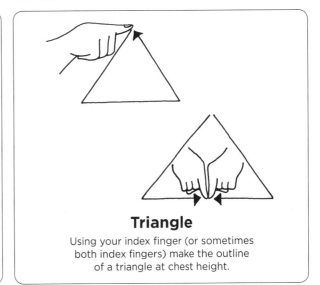

Triangle

Using your index finger (or sometimes
both index fingers) make the outline
of a triangle at chest height.

SEASONS

Calendar
Introducing ASL vocabulary for times
of the day and days of the week. 134

What's the Weather?
Learning signs for weather vocabulary 135

Numbers
Learning ASL numbers to include
with calendar activities 136

Seasonal Baskets
The Basket Game for fall,
winter, and spring 137

Opposites
Using season and weather vocabulary
to teach opposites 138

Book List 139

Songs 140

Illustrations 141

CALENDAR

This activity includes learning ASL vocabulary for words you use when you do calendar activities. Knowing these signs will help you include ASL into your daily routines.

PROCEDURE

You can use Eric Carle's book *Today Is Monday* to introduce the signs for the days of the week by signing those words as you read the book. In addition, we have found that our students love to chant and sign this ditty:

Monday we eat rice and beans.
Tuesday we eat beans and rice.
Wednesday we eat rice and beans.
Thursday we eat beans and rice.
Friday we eat rice and beans.
Saturday we eat beans and rice.
Sunday there's a change in menu,
We eat beans without the rice.

It's pretty silly, but the kids like it, and it does teach the days of the week!

Once they know this vocabulary, as you do your regular calendar activities, sign the words as you say them. You can also include signing for other calendar vocabulary. For example, try these signs:

- Afternoon
- Hour
- Morning
- Night
- Time
- Last
- Now
- When
- Day
- Calendar
- Yesterday
- Today
- Tomorrow
- Month
- Week

For example, sign "today, which one?" and have the children sign back to you the correct day of the week. Or "if today, Monday, tomorrow, which one?"

Use this vocabulary when you go over your daily schedule as well. For example, "Time for snack"; "This morning we will paint a pumpkin"; "When you go home this afternoon."

FOLLOW-UP

Continue to integrate ASL with your daily calendar routines. After the children learn the ASL numbers, you can sign the date! Months are typically finger spelled.

WHAT'S THE WEATHER?

Use this activity to introduce signs for weather and include ASL in your daily weather chart routine.

GOALS

- To learn signs for weather
- To include ASL in daily routine of checking weather
- To observe and record daily weather

MATERIALS

- Classroom weather chart

PROCEDURE

Share a book with your students, such as *What Will the Weather Be*? by Lynda Dewit, that includes weather pictures and vocabulary words. As you read the book, sign the weather vocabulary words and have the children sign them back to you. Include the following signs:

- Weather
- Ice/Freeze
- Snow
- Rain
- Clouds
- Sky
- Wind
- Clear
- Beautiful
- Sun
- Hot
- Cold
- Dark

Look through the book a second time and as you show the children the pictures, sign "what weather?" and have the children sign back the answers. Then pick someone to go to the window and check the weather outside. While that child is checking, sing and sign this song (sung to the tune of *Frère Jacques*) with the other children.

What's the weather? What's the weather?
Can you tell? Can you tell?
Go look out the window. Go look out the window.
See the weather. See the weather.

When the "weather checker" returns, have her sign the answer and then record it on your classroom weather chart.

FOLLOW-UP

Continue to do the "weather check" each day by having a student go to the window while you sing the "What's the Weather?" song and record the information on your weather chart.

NUMBERS

This activity introduces the children to counting and the numbers one through ten in ASL. ASL numbers can be used during calendar, math, board games, card games, finger plays, and many other daily activities. Learning to count in ASL also demonstrates an obvious difference between sign language and English.

GOALS

- To learn ASL numbers one through ten
- To learn to count with ASL
- To compare counting with fingers in English and in ASL

MATERIALS

- *The Handmade Counting Book* by Laura Rankin
- Cubes, counters, or other small objects that can be counted

PROCEDURE

Share the book *The Handmade Counting Book* by Laura Rankin with your students. Tell them to make the number signs as you look at the book. For the purpose of this lesson, teach only numbers one through ten. Then try counting in ASL as you sing a counting song like "Ten Little Butterflies" ("One little, two little, three little butterflies . . ."). As you sing the song, compare counting on your fingers in English with counting in ASL.

Next, place small blocks, counters, bears, or other objects to be counted in the middle of your circle. Have everyone "lock" their voices and, just as in the Basket Game, sign to the children to pick up objects from the floor. Point to a child and sign "you pick up three," or "you pick up two." Continue until every child is holding a group of objects, and then play the game in reverse by signing "Three? Who has?" or "Five? Who has?" When their number is signed, the children put their objects back.

FOLLOW-UP

You can include a review of your other sign language vocabulary as you play this game by using colored blocks and signing "yellow block, pick up two" or using school items and signing "pencil, pick up three."

Use the number signs to sign the date when you do your daily calendar activities. Sign "today, what?" and show the children how to respond by signing the day of the week, number of the day, and month. You will probably want to just finger spell the first letter of the month instead of the entire word.

SEASONAL BASKETS

In this lesson plan we present vocabulary for three different "basket games" that you can use with your seasonal curriculums.

GOALS

- To learn new ASL vocabulary for seasonal themes

MATERIALS

- Plastic bin or basket
- Small items or pictures of objects to represent the seasonal vocabulary

Fall basket:

- Leaf
- Corn
- Pumpkin
- Moon
- Dark
- Feast
- Turkey
- Ship
- Spider
- Candy
- Mask

Winter basket:

- Star
- Snowman
- Snowboard
- Candy cane
- Mountain
- Tree
- Candle
- Ski
- Snow
- Ice
- Skate
- Sled
- Light
- Family
- Gift

Spring basket:

- Umbrella
- Boots
- Rainbow
- Flower
- Rose
- Butterfly
- Bee
- Caterpillar
- Frog
- Sky

PROCEDURE

Have the children sit in a large circle with you. Place the basket in front of you and sign to the children to "lock their voices." Pick up an item from the basket, place it in the center of your circle, and show the children how to make the sign. Children watch and do the sign back. Introduce ten to fifteen signs in one sitting.

When all the objects are out in the circle, sign to the children one by one "you pick up (object)." Make eye contact with the child you are signing to and remind the other children to keep their voices "locked." If the child doesn't seem to know which item to pick up, she can sign "I forget." If she picks up the wrong object, sign "try again." Try giving her the sign for another object or help by mouthing the word. If she picks up the correct object, sign "good job" or "right." Each child gets a turn to pick up an object.

Once every child is holding an object from the basket, place the basket back in the middle of the circle. You will now ask the children in sign language to place their items back in the basket. Make the sign for the object, then sign "who has?" (for example: "Ski. Who?"). The child with that item puts it back. Continue until all items are back in the basket.

OPPOSITES

The subjects of weather and seasons provide a good opportunity to introduce the concept of opposites.

GOALS

- To review ASL for weather and seasons
- To learn about opposites
- To introduce new vocabulary

MATERIALS

None

PROCEDURE

Sit with your students in a circle and tell them you are going to say and sign some sentences to them using some of the new signs they have learned about weather and seasons.

Start by saying, "In the winter, there is a lot of snow." Sign "winter" and "snow."

Then say, "But in the summer, there is the opposite." Sign "snow, opposite, what?"

Have the children guess by signing and then sign "snow, opposite, sun."

The following are more examples:

"When it rains, we get wet."
   "Wet, opposite?"
"In summer the days are long."
   "Long, opposite?"
"In winter the animals are asleep."
   "Asleep, opposite?"

FOLLOW-UP

Have the children come up with their own "opposites." Try to encourage them to use the ASL vocabulary you all know by now, but look up signs if you need to.

Play "opposite charades" by having children stand up in front of the group and make signs, and then have the "audience" sign back the opposite. For example, one child signs "freeze" by shaking as if he is cold and the audience responds by doing the sign for "hot."

BOOKS ABOUT SEASONS, WEATHER, CALENDAR, AND COUNTING

Barrett, J. 1982. *Cloudy with a chance of meat-balls*. New York: Aladdin Library.

Baum, A. 1973. *One bright Monday morning*. New York: Random House.

Carle, E. 1969. *The very hungry caterpillar*. New York: Harper Collins.

Carle, E. 1977. *Today is Monday*. New York: Putnam Publishing.

Crews, D. 1995. *Ten black dots*. New York: Harper Trophy.

Cushman, D. 1994. *Mouse and mole and the year-round garden*. New York: WH Freeman.

Dewit, L. 1993. *What will the weather be?* New York: Harper Trophy.

Ehlert, L. 1991. *Red leaf, yellow leaf*. San Diego: Harcourt Brace & Company.

Fleming, D. 1995. *Count.* New York: Henry Holt & Co.

Gibbons, G. 1995. *The reasons for seasons*. New York: Scholastic.

McMillan, B. 1995. *Counting wildflowers*. New York: Harper Trophy.

Oppenheim, J. 1995. *Have you seen trees?* New York: Scholastic.

Provensen, A. & M. 1976. *A book of seasons*. New York: Random House.

Radin, R. 1982. *A winter place*. Boston, MA: Little, Brown & Company.

Rankin, L. 1998. *The handmade counting book.* New York: Puffin Press.

Rockwell, A. 1985. *First comes spring*. New York: HarperCollins.

Sams, C., and J. Stoick. 1999. *A stranger in the woods*. Milford, Mich.: Carl R. Sams II Photography.

Shaw, C. 1988. *It looked like spilt milk.* New York: HarperCollins.

Weniger, B., and A. Moller. 2000. *Good bread: A book of thanks.* New York: North South Books.

SONGS ABOUT SEASONS

Seasons
To: Farmer in the Dell

Autumn days are here, autumn days are here.
The leaves fall down, we dance around.
Autumn days are here.

Winter days are here, winter days are here.
Get out the sled and cover your head.
Winter days are here.

Spring days are here, spring days are here.
The flowers grow and gardeners know
That spring days are here.

Summer days are here, summer days are here.
And we all shout because school is out.
Summer days are here.

Weather Days
To: Mary Had a Little Lamb

The weather changes every day, every day,
    every day.
The weather changes every day, every day
    it's new.
Sunday is a sunny day, sunny day, sunny day.
Sunday is a sunny day, the sun shines bright
    and clear.

Monday is a rainy day, rainy day, rainy day.
Monday is a rainy day, we wear our boots and
    coats.

Tuesday is a windy day, windy day, windy day.
Tuesday is a windy day, so hang on to your hat.

Note: Add verses for the rest of the days and
different types of weather.

SIGNS FOR CALENDAR AND WEATHER

Beautiful

The right hand, fingers all touching, palm down, is held by your mouth, then moves in a counter-clockwise circle around your face opening into a "5" position; at completion of the circle, the hand returns to the closed position.

Calendar

With the fingers of the flat-palm left hand pointing up, take the right "C" hand, palm facing left, and go up and over left hand (like flipping the page of the calendar).

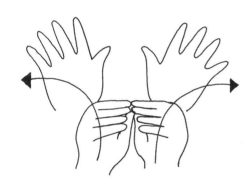

Clear

With both hands held together at chest height and fingertips touching, both hands open at the same time and spread out in either direction as if spreading rays of light.

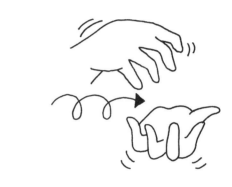

Cloud

Both hands held in "claw" shape swirl with palms facing each other.

Cold

With both hands held in "S" shape, palms facing each other in front of your body, make your arms and hands shiver.

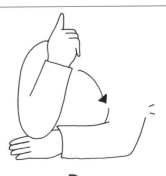

Day

The left arm is held horizontally pointing right with index finger extended. The right elbow rests on the left index finger and the right index finger points up. Move the right index finger in an arc from right to left (like the sun moving across the sky), until right index finger is touching the top of the left elbow.

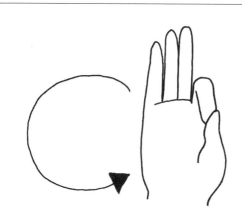

Friday

"F" hand makes a small clockwise circle.

Hot

With a right clawed hand held palm facing your mouth, quickly turn your hand palm out and open your hand like you tossed something away.

Ice/Freeze

Both hands in "5" shape, held stiff with palms down in front of your chest, contract and move slightly toward your body.

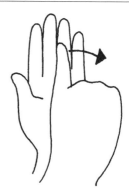

Minute/Second

Touch the left flat vertical palm with the right "D" hand index finger pointing up. For minute, move the right index finger past the left little finger; for second, move the right index finger to the left little finger.

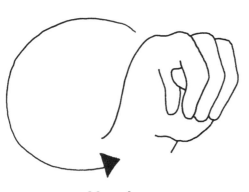

Monday

"M" hand makes a small clockwise circle.

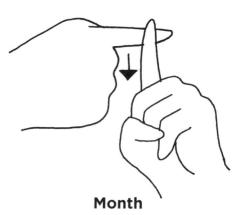

Month

The left index finger is pointing up. The right index finger begins at the top of left index finger and slides down the left finger from top to base.

Morning

Left arm flat in front with right arm lying on top. Right arm with open hand rises to upright position (sun rising in the sky).

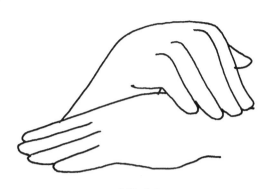

Night

With the left arm held horizontally, fingers down and flat hand pointing right, place the right forearm on the back of the left hand and move the right curved hand downward (like the sun is setting).

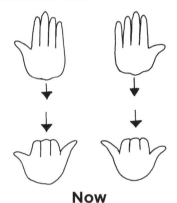

Now

Both hands, slightly bent and palms facing your body, are pulled down simultaneously and sharply a short distance ("Y" hand is often used instead of all your fingers).

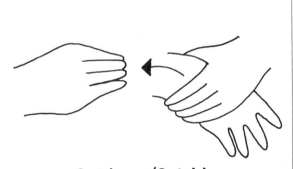

Outdoors/Outside

Your downturned open right hand, grasped loosely by your left hand, is pulled up and out of the left hand's grasp and the left hand ends in an "O" shape.

Rain

First you show the sign for water ("W" hand taps lips with index finger), then both hands in "5" shape move down wiggling (representing the rain drops).

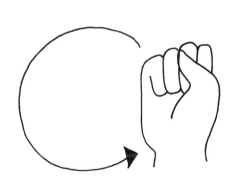

Saturday

"S" hand makes a small clockwise circle.

Sky

With your right flat hand held slightly above your head and palm facing in, move your hand in an arc from left to right.

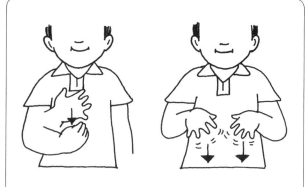

Snow

Show the sign for white (open "5" hand pulls out from chest and closes to "O" hand). Then move both palm-down open hands downward while wiggling your fingers (snow is slower to fall than rain).

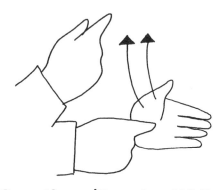

Sometimes/Once in a While

With a left flat hand held palm facing right and fingers away from your body, the right index finger touches the middle of the left palm, then the right index finger moves upward to a vertical position.

Sun

With your right index finger pointing up and hand held in "D" shape, circle in a clockwise motion, then drop fingers down and open fingers to represent the rays of light.

Sunday

Both hands flat, palms forward, move at the same time in opposite directions making a circle.

Thursday

Start with hand in "T" shape, then change to "H" and make a small clockwise circle.

Time

Use your right index finger, slightly curved to tap on the back of your left wrist (like it is your watch) several times.

Tomorrow

With a right "A" hand, thumb pointing up, move your hand forward from right cheek out a few inches from your face.

Today (Now + Day)

Begin with the sign for now (both hands, slightly bent and palms facing your body, are pulled down simultaneously and sharply a short distance; "Y" hand is often used instead of all your fingers). And then do the sign for day. (The left arm is held horizontally pointing right with index finger extended. The right elbow rests on the left index finger and the right index finger points up. Move the right index finger in an arc from right to left [like the sun moving across the sky], until right index finger is touching the top of the left elbow.)

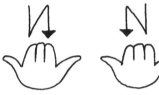

or

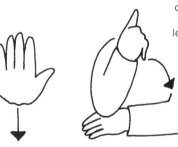

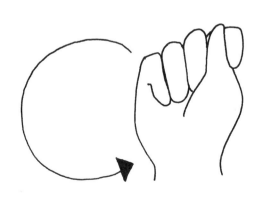

Tuesday

"T" hand makes a small clockwise circle.

Weather

With both hands held in "W," facing each other, pivot up and down from your wrists.

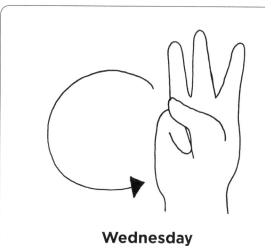

Wednesday

"W" hand makes a small clockwise circle.

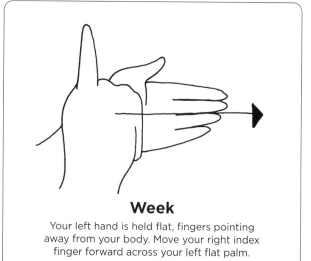

Week

Your left hand is held flat, fingers pointing away from your body. Move your right index finger forward across your left flat palm.

Wind

Both hands held in the "5" position, with palms facing each other, sway gracefully back and forth in unison. You can blow air from your mouth at the same time, to produce the wind.

or

Yesterday

With a right "Y" hand, palm facing forward on the right side of your chin, make an arc backward toward your ear.

Numbers
(The numbers are self-explanatory. Once you get to 16, you show the ones column number and then turn your wrist to show the 10s column.)

How Many?
Both hands held in "B" shape, palms down, are turned up and changed to "O" shape, then fingers flick open.

Candy

Index finger touches side of face by molar teeth and twists (like a cavity is there).

Corn

The right index finger is held across the front of lower lip and turned as if eating corn off the cob.

Dark

Both open hands are held in front of your face, then they move toward each other in a slight downward arch and cross (shutting out the light).

Fall (season)

Hold your left arm at an angle across your chest (it represents a tree branch). With your right open "5" hand, index fingers touching outside of left forearm, slide your right hand down representing the leaves falling from the branch.

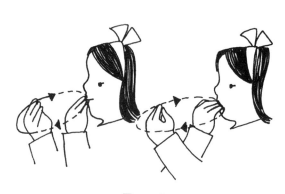

Feast

Both hands' fingers alternately come to mouth as if placing food in the mouth repeatedly.

Leaf

The left "5" hand is held flat, fingers pointing away from body and slightly down (this hand is the leaf) and the right index finger touches at right wrist.

Mask

With both hands flat and held in front of your face, palms in and little fingers touching, swing your hands open showing your face.

Moon

The right "C" hand (or sometimes you see only the thumb and index finger being used) is held at the side of your right cheek, then arches away from your face and over your head ending with "C" hand above your head and slightly to the side.

Pumpkin

With a "C" hand, show the sign for orange. Hold the right "C" hand at your mouth and open and close deliberately as if squeezing an orange. Then hold your hands apart as if holding a big pumpkin. Next, with your left hand in the "S" shape, take the middle right finger and flick the back of your left hand like you are knocking away the seeds.

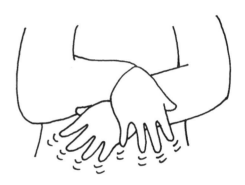

Spider

With both hands held in "5" shape, crossed at the wrist with palms down, your eight fingers become the legs of the spider.

Turkey

A right "Q" hand, palm facing down, shakes back and forth under your chin.

Candle

The left "5" hand is held above the right index finger. The left hand pivots back and forth like the flame blowing slightly.

Candy Cane

First show the sign for candy (index finger touches side of face by molar teeth and twists like a cavity is there). Then hold the left hand in the "O" shape and with a right "F" hand put fingers in left "O" and pull out and arch over like the shape of a candy cane.

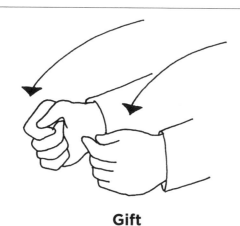

Gift

With both hands held palms facing each other with index fingers bent and touching thumbs, move both hands forward in a slight arch away from your chest.

Ice/Freeze

Both hands in "5" shape, held stiff with palms down in front of your chest, contract and move slightly toward your body.

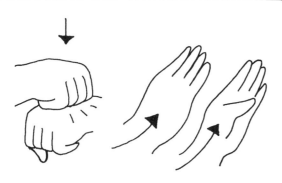

Mountain

With both hands closed, use right hand to strike the back of left (rock), then both hands move up simultaneously to show the mountain.

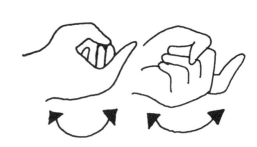

Skate

With both hands held in "X" shape with palms facing up, make the movement of skating, pulling out to either side alternately.

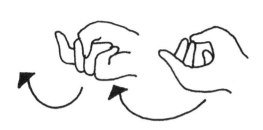

Ski

With both hands held in "X" shape, palms facing up, arch both hands forward simultaneously as if skiing down a hill.

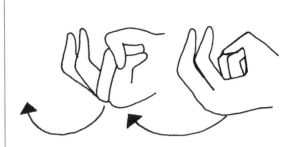

Sled

With both hands held in "V" shape, palms facing up (like the runners on the bottom of the sled), arch both hands forward simultaneously as if going down a hill.

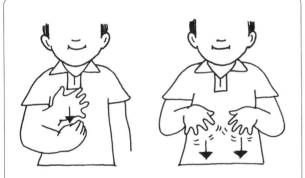

Snow

Show the sign for white (open "5" hand pulls out from chest and closes to "O" hand). Then move both palm-down open hands downward while wiggling your fingers (snow is slower to fall than rain).

Snowboard

Left hand is held flat, palm down, and right "V" hand is held in a downward position on the back of left (like the fingers are the legs of the snowboarder). Left hand moves forward carrying right hand as if going down the mountain.

Snowman

Show the sign for white (open "5" hand pulls out from chest and closes to "O" hand). Then move both palm-down open hands downward while wiggling your fingers (snow is slower to fall than rain). The sign for man is shown by holding a "B" hand palm down across forehead as if grabbing the bill of a cap and then moving down in "5" shape and touching chest with thumb.

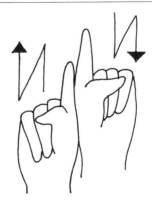

Star

Both index fingers stand straight up in front of you and brush against each other as they reach up toward the sky.

Tree

While right elbow rests in the palm of the
left hand, right fingers wiggle a bit.

Winter

Hold both hands in "S" shape in front of
your chest and shake them, while tightening
your body to look cold.

SIGNS FOR SPRING

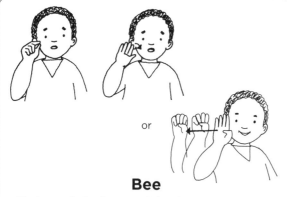

or

Bee

Pinch your index finger and thumb of your right hand
together and have it touch the side of your right
cheek (like a sting) then quickly swat it away.
OR: Use a "B" hand on your right cheek and
pull it away changing into an "E" hand.

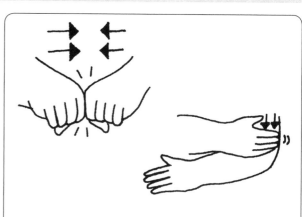

Boot

With both hands held in "S" shape tap together
for shoe, then the right "5" hand taps left arm
above wrist (tall shoe = boot).

Bug/Insect

With your right hand in "3" shape, rest your thumb on the tip of your nose and bend your index and middle finger a few times.

Butterfly

Cross your hands in front of your chest, palms facing in, and lock your thumbs together. Flap your fingers like wings.

Caterpillar

The right index finger crawls up the left forearm like a caterpillar.

Flower

With the fingers of your right hand cupped in a flat "O" shape, place your fingertips under each nostril separately.

Frog

The right "3" hand is held below your chin and the fingers open and close (like a frog croaking).

Grass

With an open "5" hand, palm facing your body, hand in front of lips moves up a few times (like smelling newly cut grass).

Kite

With both hands, pull on imaginary
string while looking up.

Rainbow

Tap your lips with the fingers from your open right hand,
then place all your right fingertips into your left palm,
pull up and let fingers spread as they arch over (like
spreading the colors of the rainbow across the sky).

Rose

Right "R" hand goes from right
to left side of your nose.

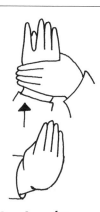

Spring/Grow

The open fingers of the right hand come up and
through the left "C" hand, opening as it comes up
(left hand the ground, right hand the plant or flower).

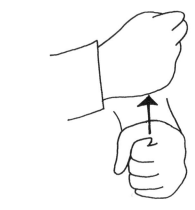

Umbrella

With both hands closed, hold the right over the left and
raise the right hand a bit (like opening an umbrella).

Asleep

Pull your open hand down over your face. As your hand moves down, the fingers and eyes close simultaneously, ending with your head slightly tilted forward.

Awake

Pinch your index finger and thumb together at both sides of your face next to your eyes. As the fingers open, so do your eyes.

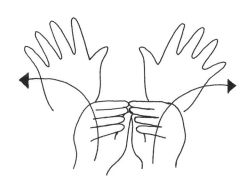

Clear

With both hands held together at chest height and fingertips touching, both hands open at the same time and spread out in either direction as if spreading rays of light.

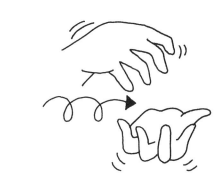

Cloud

Both hands held in "claw" shape swirl with palms facing each other.

Cold

With both hands held in "S" shape, palms facing each other in front of your body, make your arms and hands shiver.

Dark

Both open hands are held in front of your face, then they move toward each other in a slight downward arch and cross (shutting out the light).

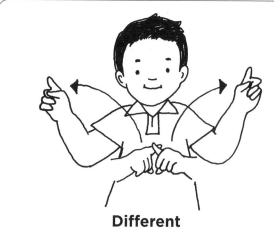

Different

Make two "D" hands with your index fingers crossing, then separate and return the fingers several times.

Dry

With an "X" shape right index finger, pull your finger across your chin a few times.

Hot

With a right clawed hand held palm facing your mouth, quickly turn your hand palm out and open your hand like you tossed something away.

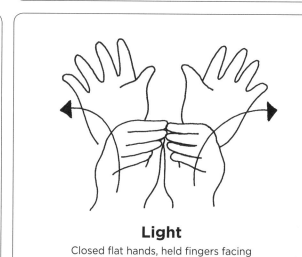

Light

Closed flat hands, held fingers facing each other, spring open into "5" hands.

Opposites

Both hands in "1" position are held palms in, fingers touching, then pulled apart.

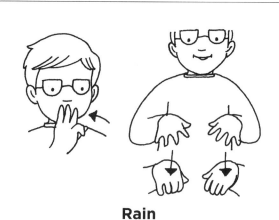

Rain

First you show the sign for water ("W" hand taps lips with index finger), then both hands in "5" shape move down wiggling (representing the rain drops).

Summer

Your right curved index finger moves from left to right across your forehead ending in the "X" shape.

Sun

With your right index finger pointing up and hand held in "D" shape, circle in a clockwise motion, then drop fingers down and open fingers to represent the rays of light.

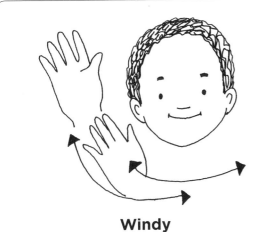

Windy

Both hands open, palms facing each other, swoop through the air a few times.

Winter

Hold both hands in "S" shape in front of your chest and shake them, while tightening your body to look cold.

COMMUNITY
HELPERS

The Basket Game
Introducing the vocabulary 160

Operator
Using the vocabulary and
practicing ASL sentences. 161

Safe/Not Safe
Learn safety signs and about
safe and unsafe situations 162

Helping Our Deaf Friends
Learn about how to help a deaf or
hard-of-hearing person in an emergency. 163

Red Light/Green Light
Based on the children's game,
but using basic safety signs. 164

Book List 165

Songs 166

Illustrations. 167

THE BASKET GAME: COMMUNITY HELPERS

GOALS

- To introduce new sign language vocabulary
- To review signs

MATERIALS

- A basket or plastic bin
- Small objects that represent sign vocabulary you want the children to learn

For "community helper" vocabulary, use any small toy people and vehicles that you have in your classroom. Begin with as many new signs as you think your students can learn in one session. If you have followed this curriculum in the order presented, then by this time your students will be quite proficient signers and can probably learn more than fifteen new signs at a time. If this seems like too much vocabulary for one game, you can introduce some during another session.

Vocabulary for introducing community helper signs:

- Bus
- Fire truck
- Ambulance
- Police car
- Ferry boat
- Tow truck
- Library
- Doctor
- Post office
- Veterinarian
- Farmer
- Traffic light
- Police
- Firefighter
- Dentist
- Teacher
- Mail carrier
- Stop sign

PROCEDURE

Explain with your voice before you begin that this will be a "no voice" activity and that the children will need to watch you carefully to know what to do.

Have the children sit in a large circle with you. Place the basket in front of you and sign to the children to "lock their voices." Pick up an item from the basket, place it in the center of your circle, and show the children how to make the sign. Children watch and do the sign back.

When all the objects are out in the circle, sign to the children one by one "you pick up (object)." Make eye contact with the child you are signing to and remind the other children to keep their voices "locked." If the child doesn't seem to know which item to pick up, he can sign "I forget." If he picks up the wrong object, sign "try again." Try giving him the sign for another object or help by mouthing the word. If he picks up the correct object, sign "good job" or "right." Each child gets a turn to pick up an object.

Once every child is holding an object from the basket, place the basket back in the middle of the circle. You will now ask the children in sign language to place their items back in the basket. Make the sign for the object, and then sign "who has?" (for example, "Tow truck. Who has?") The child with that item puts it back. Continue until all items are back in the basket.

OPERATOR

This is based on the traditional children's game, but instead of whispering a message in someone's ear, the children sign the message down a row and see what message ends up at the end. This game increases ASL sentence skills and vocabulary.

GOALS

- To practice community helper signs
- To enhance signing skills
- To practice ASL sentences

MATERIALS

None

PROCEDURE

Have the children sit in a straight line, one behind the other, so they are looking at the back of another child. Use the community helper vocabulary to sign a message to the last person in the line. For example, "firefighter go in fire truck" or "cars drive on ferry boat." Make sure no one else can see what you are signing. Then have that child turn around and sign the same message to the child in front of her. Continue signing the message down the line until the first child in line gets it. Have her show you the signed message she received and see if it is the same one you gave.

NOTE

This is a really fun game and, like the traditional "Operator" game, the message is rarely the same and is oftentimes quite ridiculous! This game should be played when the children are competent expressive signers. They sometimes need help with remembering the correct signs.

FOLLOW-UP

Continue using your community helper vocabulary to think of new messages.

Give other children a chance to think of the original message to send down the line.

SAFE/NOT SAFE

In this lesson the children learn ASL vocabulary for safety signs, and the teachers role-play different situations for the children. The children make decisions about whether or not the situations are safe.

GOALS

- Learn ASL vocabulary for "safety" signs.
- Learn about safe and unsafe behavior.

MATERIALS

None

PROCEDURE

Talk to the children about the different ways we keep ourselves safe. Introduce the new "safety" vocabulary, including the following:

- Safe
- Not safe
- Blood
- Bandage
- Help
- Hurt
- Stop
- Emergency
- 911
- Danger
- Break
- Sick
- Fire

Then role-play different situations with another teacher or volunteer.

Use your voice to talk about what the situation is, but also include the new ASL vocabulary. For example, have several children crowd into a small area of the classroom, like the listening center. Pretend one child gets pushed and falls down. Sign "not safe" and "hurt." Or pretend to run through the classroom, not looking where you are going, and trip over a chair. Sign "not safe" and "danger."

Afterward, ask the children if the situation/ behavior was safe or not safe. Use the signs and have them sign the answer back to you. Ask them how to change the situation to be "safe."

FOLLOW-UP

Role-play different unsafe situations or behaviors that you observe going on in your own classroom. Then ask the children how you could make the behaviors "safe."

HELPING OUR DEAF FRIENDS

This activity helps the hearing children in your classroom understand different ways to communicate with deaf or hard-of-hearing people and how to be helpful in emergency situations.

This is a very important lesson to include if you have deaf or hard-of-hearing students in your class.

GOALS

- To learn to get the attention of people who are deaf
- To learn "safety" signs to use in an emergency

MATERIALS

- Props for role play situations

PROCEDURE

Talk with your students about how they get the attention of someone who is deaf. By now they may have had several interactions with deaf volunteers or other children in the class. They may be familiar with tapping a deaf person to get his or her attention, banging on the table or floor, or flicking the lights on and off.

Tell them that you are going to talk about what to do in an emergency to help our deaf friends.

For example, if the fire alarm goes off, would our deaf friends hear it and know what to do? How could we help them? You can mention that most alarms have lights that flick on and off, but show the children how you could tap your deaf friend and sign "fire," "alarm," or "smoke."

Or if one of our deaf friends is hurt, we can sign "what's wrong?" or "need help?"

Have the children try to think of other situations in which they might need to help a friend who does not hear and maybe does not speak. Try to include this vocabulary:

- Alarm
- Smoke
- Fire
- Sick
- Danger
- Bandage
- Help
- What's wrong?

FOLLOW-UP

Encourage your students to interact with deaf people they might see in their community. Our students often came to school with stories about meeting someone who is deaf and were very excited about using their sign language to interact.

LESSON PLAN

RED LIGHT/GREEN LIGHT

This is based on the traditional children's game, but incorporates signing for "red light, stop" and "green light, go."

GOALS

- To practice community helper signs
- To play a large-motor game in ASL
- To have children use expressive signing

MATERIALS

None

PROCEDURE

This game is best played outdoors or in a very large open space and is played using only ASL. The teacher is the "traffic light" and the students can choose what kind of "transportation" they want to be. Ask them to sign to you what they are: "fire truck," "tow truck," "bus," "car," "ambulance," etc. The "traffic light" stands several yards away from the "transportation vehicles" and signals them in sign language when they can move. She signs "green light, go" or "red light, stop!" As the students move, they make the noise of their vehicle and make the sign. When all the vehicles get to the traffic light, choose a student to be the new traffic signal and go back and start again!

NOTE

To make the "choosing vehicles" go faster and easier, you can pass out necklace cards with the names and signs for the vehicles. The children can wear these signs as they play, and then trade for each new game.

Make sure the children understand they have to watch the traffic light with their eyes for the signing signal to stop or go!

164 Sign to Learn

BOOKS ABOUT COMMUNITY HELPERS

Arnold, C. 1982. *Who works here?* New York: Scholastic.

Baer, E. 1990. *This is the way we go to school.* New York: Scholastic.

Barken, J. 1990. *Whiskerville fire station.* Wiltshire, U.K.: Child's Play International.

Barken, J. 1998. *Whiskerville post office.* Wiltshire, U.K.: Child's Play International.

Bloom, S. 2001. *The bus for us.* Honesdale, Pa.: Boyds Mills Press.

Bunting, E. 1994. *Smoky night.* Orlando, Fla.: Voyager Books.

Crew, D. 1984. *School bus.* New York: Harper Trophy.

Crew, D. 1991. *Truck.* New York: Harper Trophy.

Henderson, K. 1989. *I can be a farmer.* New York: Scholastic.

Henkes, K. 1987. *Once around the block.* New York: HarperCollins.

Leaf, M. 1961. *Safety can be fun.* New York: HarperCollins.

Linn, M. 1988. *A trip to the dentist.* New York: HarperCollins.

Linn, M. 1988. *A trip to the doctor.* New York: HarperCollins.

Moss, M. 1994. *Mel's diner.* New York: Troll.

Thomas, P. 2003. *I can be safe.* Hauppauge, N.Y.: Barron's Educational Series.

Williams, V. 1984. *A chair for my mother.* New York: Harper Trophy.

Ziefert, H. 1986. *No, no, Nicky.* New York: Penguin Books.

SONGS ABOUT COMMUNITY HELPERS

Walking Down the Street
To: London Bridge

When I was walking down the street, down the
 street, down the street,
A community helper I did meet.
Who did I meet?

A firefighter was on my street, on my street,
 on my street.
A firefighter was on my street.
Who did you meet?

A doctor was on her street, on her street, on
 her street.
A doctor was on her street,
Who did you meet?

Note: After singing "Who did you meet?" at the end
of the second and subsequent verses, point to a
child to say and sign a community helper.

Community Helpers
To: Old MacDonald Had a Farm

In our community we have helpers,
Helping all day long.
In our community we have a teacher,
Helping all day long.
With a lesson here, and a lesson there,
Here a lesson, there a lesson,
All day long she teaches lessons.

In our community we have helpers,
Helping all day long.
In our community we have a mail carrier,
Helping all day long.
With a delivery here and a delivery there,
Here a delivery, there a delivery,
All day long she makes deliveries.

In our community we have helpers,
Helping all day long.

Note: Add new verses with the ASL vocabulary for
community helpers.

SIGNS FOR COMMUNITY HELPERS

Ambulance

With the fingers of your right hand extended above your head, rotate hand as if it were the sirens' flashing lights.

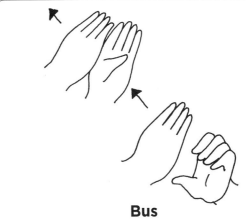

Bus

Both hands touch in "B" shape, palms facing opposite directions; then pull hands apart making left hand into a "C" shape.

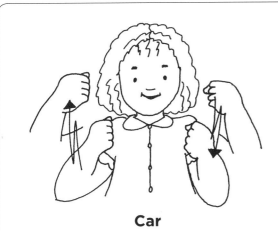

Car

Have both hands in "S" shape resemble holding the steering wheel of the car (move up and down).

City/Town/Community

With both hands flat, fingertips touching resemble many rooftops.

Dentist

Right index finger taps teeth. Then palms facing each other move down the sides of your body.

Doctor

With left hand closed and palm up, the right "M" hand taps on left wrist as if taking a pulse.

Farmer

With a flat "5" hand, touch the right side of your mouth and then the left, then with palms facing each other move down the sides of your body.

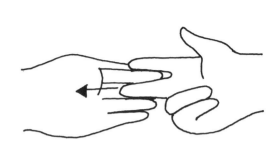

Ferry Boat

First a right "3" hand is used as a classifier to represent the car driving onto a left cupped hand, then right hand joins left and now both hands are cupped (to show boat). Then with right hand, thumb up, it goes back and forth like the boat crossing the water.

Firefighter

Place a right "B" hand, palm facing out, above your forehead.

Librarian

"L" hand makes a circle, then both flat hands, palms facing each other, move down the sides of your body.

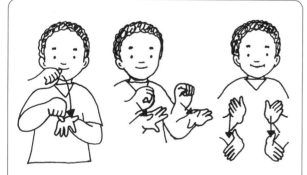

Mail Carrier

With right hand held with thumb up, touch thumb to lips (like licking a stamp), then thumb touches middle of left open palm. With both hands held open before the body, close simultaneously. Then, with palms facing each other, move down the sides of your body.

Police

With a right "C" hand tap on your chest where the badge would be.

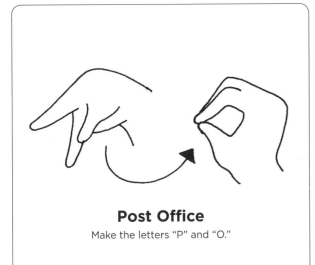

Post Office

Make the letters "P" and "O."

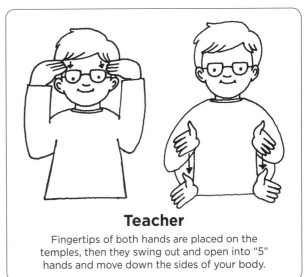

Teacher

Fingertips of both hands are placed on the temples, then they swing out and open into "5" hands and move down the sides of your body.

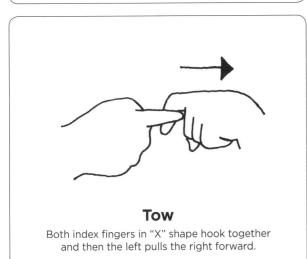

Tow

Both index fingers in "X" shape hook together and then the left pulls the right forward.

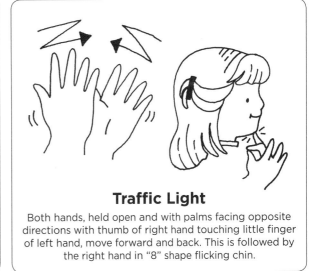

Traffic Light

Both hands, held open and with palms facing opposite directions with thumb of right hand touching little finger of left hand, move forward and back. This is followed by the right hand in "8" shape flicking chin.

Truck

Have both hands in "S" shape resemble holding the steering wheel of the truck.

Veterinarian

Fingers spell out V E T.

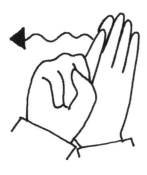

Alarm

With the right index finger extended, the right hand strikes the left palm and then wiggles away.

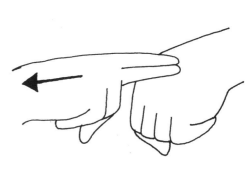

Bandage

The right "U" hand slides across the back of the left hand.

Blood

The right index finger touches your lower lip (the sign for red), then the right hand fingers wiggle over the back of your left hand moving down as they go (like blood running out and down).

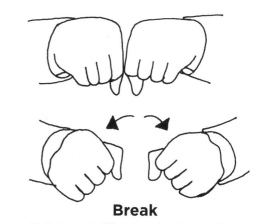

Break

Both hands in "S" shape, thumbs touching, twist apart sharply and pull outward.

Burn

Finger spell B U R N. OR: Both hands in "5" position are held palms facing body and fingers wiggle moving up and down alternately.

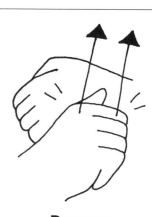

Danger

The right closed hand (or fist) strikes the back of the left closed hand (or fist) a few times in an upward motion.

Emergency 911

Sign the numbers 9-1-1.

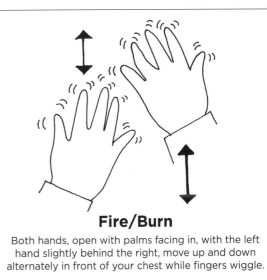

Fire/Burn

Both hands, open with palms facing in, with the left hand slightly behind the right, move up and down alternately in front of your chest while fingers wiggle.

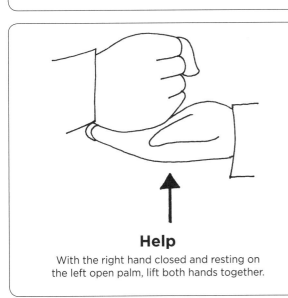

Help

With the right hand closed and resting on the left open palm, lift both hands together.

Hurt

Both index fingers face each other and twist almost touching.

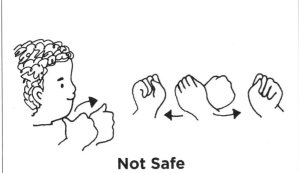

Not Safe

The right thumb is tucked under the chin and pulled forward, then with both hands in "S" shape and crossed in front of your body, swing hands apart and out facing (not + safe).

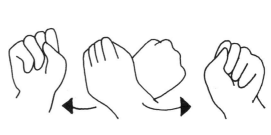

Safety/Safe

With both hands in "S" shape and crossed in front of your body, swing hands apart and out-facing.

Shock

The right index finger touches the right temple, then both hands drop in front of your chest and pull in and stiffen (like the sign for ice).

Sick

The right middle finger touches the forehead and the left index finger touches the stomach. Let your tongue hang out a bit.

Smoke

The right index finger draws a line across your forehead, then both hands clawed, palms facing each other, circle around and the right hand rises up like smoke rising.

Sting

The right index finger and thumb pinch together and strike the back of the left hand.

Stop

With both hands open, the right hand with little finger down strikes left hand.

Telephone

The right hand is in the "Y" shape with the thumb held near the ear and the little finger by the mouth.

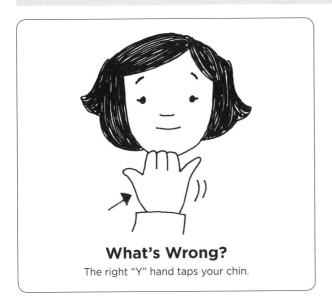

What's Wrong?

The right "Y" hand taps your chin.

ANIMALS

The Basket Game
Introducing animal vocabulary 176

The Magic Box
Practice animal signs and act
like animals 177

Hidden Animals
Practice expressive animal signs. 178

Animal Go and Find
Searching game 179

Who Lives Here?
Sorting game with animal vocabulary. 180

Book List 181

Songs 181

Illustrations. 182

THE BASKET GAME: ANIMALS

GOALS

- To introduce new sign language vocabulary
- To review signs

MATERIALS

- A basket or plastic bin
- Small objects that represent sign vocabulary you want the children to learn

For "animal" vocabulary, use any small animal toys that you have in your classroom. Begin with as many new signs as you think your students can learn in one session. If you have followed this curriculum in the order presented, then this will be your final unit. By this time your students will be quite proficient signers and can probably learn more than fifteen new signs at a time. If this seems like too much vocabulary for one game, you can introduce some during another session.

Vocabulary for introducing animal signs:

- Animal
- Bear
- Bee
- Bird
- Butterfly
- Cat
- Chicken
- Cow
- Dog
- Fish
- Frog
- Horse
- Lion
- Monkey
- Mouse
- Pig
- Rabbit
- Sheep
- Snake
- Spider
- Turkey
- Turtle
- Wolf

PROCEDURE

Explain with your voice before you begin that this will be a "no voice" activity and that the children will need to watch you carefully to know what to do.

Have the children sit in a large circle with you. Place the basket in front of you and sign to the children to "lock their voices." Pick up an item from the basket, place it in the center of your circle, and show the children how to make the sign. Children watch and do the sign back. Introduce ten to fifteen signs in one sitting.

When all the objects are out in the circle, sign to the children one by one "you pick up (object)." Make eye contact with the child you are signing to and remind the other children to keep their voices "locked." If the child doesn't seem to know which item to pick up, she can sign "I forget." If she picks up the wrong object, sign "try again." Try giving her the sign for another object or help by mouthing the word. If she picks up the correct object, sign "good job" or "right." Each child gets a turn to pick up an object.

Once every child is holding an object from the basket, place the basket back in the middle of the circle. You will now ask the children in sign language to place their items back in the basket. Make the sign for the object, and then sign "who has?" (for example, "Wolf. Who?"). The child with that item puts it back. Continue until all items are back in the basket.

LESSON PLAN

THE MAGIC BOX

This is a game that a volunteer from the Deaf community brought to the classroom. It is a pantomiming and signing game that gives the children opportunities to be expressive with their bodies and faces. It is also a good way to review sign language vocabulary words.

GOALS

- To use acting, facial expressions, and body movements to act out specific animals
- To review sign language vocabulary for animals
- To exercise imagination and creativity

MATERIALS

None

PROCEDURE

Sitting in a circle with the whole group or a small group of children, say, "I have a magic box that I want to share with all of you." Pretend to hold a box in front of you. Explain that in your magic box there are many animals. Pretend to look through the box and pull something out. Then use your body to move like the animal and make your face look like the animal's face. For example, if you choose dog as your animal, you might shake your imaginary tail and pant. The children guess what is in the box by signing the answer. Pass the box around so each child can have a turn pulling something out and acting it out for the class to guess.

NOTE

Make sure that the children are using sign language to guess what is in the box and that they are doing the signs correctly. Watch to see what the children choose to act out (i.e., if they all do something similar or if they can be creative).

Some of the children will need help thinking of what to pull out of the box. If a child does not want a turn, he needs only to "pass the box" to the next person.

FOLLOW-UP

This game can be played again and again. It needs no materials and can be done with many variations.

You can use this game as a good review of other sign language vocabulary like colors, clothes, or feelings. For example, there are feelings in the magic box; you can pretend to put on a mask, and then make a face to illustrate the feeling.

HIDDEN ANIMALS

This game encourages children to use expressive signing and also sign full ASL sentences. It illustrates the difference between ASL and English sentence structure.

GOALS

- To review animal signs
- To introduce new animal vocabulary
- To have children practice expressive signing

MATERIALS

- Toy animals from the Basket Game

PROCEDURE

Choose three toy animals at a time. Have the children sit in a circle on the floor with their hands behind their backs and their eyes closed. As you walk around the outside of the circle, holding the three animals, sing this song:

I'm hiding the (name of animal), I'm hiding the_____, I'm hiding the_____, where no one can see.

As you sing and walk around the circle, place an animal in three children's hands.

Now have the children open their eyes, but keep their hands behind their backs so no one knows who holds the animals. Then sing and sign the following:

Who has the (name of animal)? (Sign the animal first, then "who has?")

Then the child who has that animal will sing and sign:

"I have the (name of animal)." ("[Name of animal], I have.")

Continue with the next two animals until everyone can see.

NOTE

Encourage all the children to do the signs for the animals when you find out who has them. Children who do not want a turn can sign "no thanks."

Continue playing with three new animals each time you sing the song, until everyone has had a turn to hold an animal.

FOLLOW-UP

This game can also be played to review other sign language vocabulary. Just use the objects from your Basket Games.

Let the children take turns hiding the objects and singing and signing the song.

LESSON PLAN

ANIMAL GO AND FIND

In this game the children work in teams to identify sign illustrations of animals and locate the toy animals in the classroom.

GOALS

- To "read" a sign illustration
- To work in cooperative teams to complete a task
- To practice animal sign language vocabulary

MATERIALS

- Toy animals
- Copies of ASL illustrations for animal signs

PROCEDURE

Hide the toy animals in different places around your classroom. Place them where they can be seen, not inside drawers or cabinets. Divide your class into groups of four or five children. Give each group copies of the signs for six different animals. You may use the illustrations we have provided in this book, or from another ASL dictionary. However, make sure the illustration shows just the sign, not a picture of the animal or the printed name. Send the teams of children to "go find" their animals. When they return with all six, give them some "deaf applause" by waving hands in the air.

NOTE

It is good to have adult helpers with this game, although we have found that the children are quite capable of understanding the illustrations even the first time they see them. This is good practice for them to use an ASL dictionary to learn new signs on their own.

Try to balance your teams with children who are strong sign language learners and those who need extra help.

FOLLOW-UP

You can play several times by exchanging the sign illustrations between the teams and hiding the animals in different places.

When the children return to the circle with their animal toys, ask each team to sign the ones they found: "What find?"

This game can also be played with the other sign language vocabulary objects like food, family members, and community helpers.

WHO LIVES HERE?

In this game the children sort animals by where they live and use the animal signs to communicate their answers.

GOALS

- To review animal signs
- To learn new signs for animal habitats
- To learn to sort items into specific groups

MATERIALS

- Toy animals
- Sign language illustrations for forest (many trees), zoo, farm, and ocean

PROCEDURE

Talk with the children about how different animals live in different environments.

Show the children the signs for forest, zoo, farm, and ocean. Place the illustrations for these signs on the floor in the middle of your circle. Bring out your toy animals and review the signs for the animal names. Then point to one of the habitats and say and sign "who lives here?" Have the children sign back to you which animals they think live in that habitat. When you agree, place the animal on that illustration. Continue until you have "homes" for all the animals.

NOTE

You can enlarge and copy the signs we have included in this book, or use another ASL dictionary. For this game it is helpful to have the word and/or a picture of the word printed on the sign language illustration card.

FOLLOW-UP

You can add new animals and habitats to fit the interests of the children in your class or any particular curriculum units you are teaching.

BOOKS ABOUT ANIMALS

Aarderna, V. 1975. *Why mosquitos buzz in people's ears*. Hong Kong: South China Printing Co.

Aliki, 1999. *My visit to the zoo*. New York: Harper Trophy.

Arnosky, J. 2000. *I see animals hiding*. New York: Scholastic.

Cherry, L. 1990. *The great Kapok tree*. Orlando, Fla.: Voyager Books.

Cole, W. 1958. *I went to the animal fair*. Cleveland, Ohio: World Publishing.

Dodds, S. 1999. *Old MacDonald had a farm*. Cambridge, Mass.: Candlewick Press.

Ehlert, L. 1989. *Color zoo*. New York: HarperCollins.

Fain, K. 1993. *Hand signs: A sign language alphabet*. New York: Scholastic.

Guarino, D. 1989. *Is your mama a llama?* New York: Scholastic.

Heller, R. 1981. *Chickens aren't the only ones*. New York: Putnam.

Martin, B. 1967. *Brown bear, brown bear, what do you see?* New York: Henry Holt & Co.

Martin, B. 1991. *Polar bear, polar bear, what do you hear?* New York: Henry Holt & Co.

Wise-Brown, M. 1991. *The big red barn*. New York: Harper Trophy.

SONGS ABOUT ANIMALS

Around the Zoo
To: The Muffin Man

If I were a chimpanzee, a chimpanzee,
   a chimpanzee,
If I were a chimpanzee, I'd swing around
   the zoo.

If I were a crocodile, a crocodile, a crocodile,
If I were a crocodile, I'd snap around the zoo.

If I were a fruit bat, a fruit bat, a fruit bat,
If I were a fruit bat, I'd hang upside down
   at the zoo.

Note: Change the animal and the action to add more verses!

Animal Habitats
To: Bingo

There was an animal that lived in the jungle
And tiger was his name-o.
T-I-G-E-R, T-I-G-E-R, T-I-G-E-R
And tiger was his name-o.

There was an animal that lived on the farm
And horse was her name-o.
H-O-R-S-E, H-O-R-S-E, H-O-R-S-E.
And horse was her name-o.

There was an animal that lived in the ocean
And whale was her name-o.
W-H-A-L-E, W-H-A-L-E, W-H-A-L-E,
And whale was her name-o.

Note: Finger spell the animal names and change the habitat and animal to add more verses.

Animal

Fingertips of both hands touch either side of the chest and rock in and out a few times.

Bear

Cross your arms in front of your chest with palms facing in and open and close your fingers like they are clawing.

or

Bee

Pinch your index finger and thumb of your right hand together and have it touch the side of your right cheek (like a sting) then quickly swat it away. OR: Use a "B" hand on your right cheek and pull it away changing into an "E" hand.

Bird

With your right index finger and thumb, make a beak open and shut by your mouth.

Bug/Insect

With your right hand in "3" shape, rest your thumb on the tip of your nose and bend your index and middle finger a few times.

Butterfly

Cross your hands in front of your chest, palms facing in, and lock your thumbs together. Flap your fingers like wings.

Cat
Pinch your index fingers and thumbs together leaving all your other fingers standing tall (to be whiskers), then place your thumb and index fingers on either side of your nose and pinch and pull out a short distance (you can use one or both hands).

Caterpillar
The right index finger crawls up the left forearm like a caterpillar.

Chicken
With your right index finger and thumb pointing forward, open and close at your lips, then your right index finger in "X" shape scratches at the middle of your left palm (like pecking for food).

Cow
With your right "Y" hand place your thumb by your right temple and turn back and forth (you can use one or both hands).

Dog
With your right hand pat your right knee and snap your fingers to call the dog.

Farm
With an open right hand the thumb touches the right side of your mouth and then the left.

Fish

The open right hand, palm facing your body,
swims across in front of your chest.

Frog

The right "3" hand is held below your chin and the
fingers open and close (like a frog croaking).

Go

Both index fingers move in an arch
together away from body.

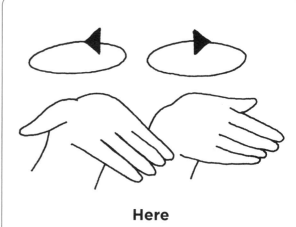

Here

With both hands open and palms up,
make small circles in front of your chest.

Hide

Right "A" hand, thumb touching
lips, slides under left curved hand,
palm down (quiet and under).

Horse

Both hands in "U" form are placed on either side
of your head and the index and middle fingers
move forward and back (the ears of a horse).

Lion

With a right claw hand held fingers pointing down and palm facing body, pull your hand up and over your head.

Live

Both "L" shape hands slide up either side of your chest.

Monkey

With both "5" hands, fingertips pointing in toward armpit and thumbs pointing out, scratch a few times next to your armpits.

Mouse

The right index finger brushes past your nose.

Ocean

The "W" shape right hand taps your lips (water), and then both hands, palms facing down, make waves with fingers going up and down simultaneously.

Pig

The right "B" hand is placed palm down under your chin and the fingers flap up and down as one.

Rabbit

Both hands held in "U" shape are turned backward and held on either side of the head, then fingers flop up and down like rabbit ears. OR: With both hands in "U" shape and wrists crossed in front of your chest, fingers flop like ears.

Sheep

Hold your left arm out in front of your body, and with your right hand in a "V" shape, palm facing up, move along your left arm with "V" fingers opening and shutting (like cutting the wool).

Snake

With a curved right "V" hand, palm facing down, have your arm and hand slither like a snake (the "V" hand is the head).

Spider

With both hands held in "5" shape, crossed at the wrist with palms down, your eight fingers become the legs of the spider.

Turkey

A right "Q" hand, palm facing down, shakes back and forth under your chin.

Turtle

With a left "A" hand turned so that the thumb is up, take your right hand and cover your left hand with the little finger away from your body. The thumb of your left hand pulls in and out and looks around like the head of a turtle.

Who

Thumb touches chin, and index finger bounces a bit by your mouth.

Wolf

With an open right hand, palm facing in, begin with fingers open around mouth and nose, then pull out from face and close fingers.

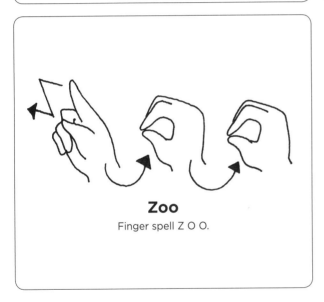

Zoo

Finger spell Z O O.

AMERICAN SIGN LANGUAGE ILLUSTRATION INDEX

Again 42, 73
Alarm 170
Alphabet A-Z 34
Ambulance 167
American Sign Language 28
Animal 182
Apple 110
Arm 77
Art 95
Asleep 155
Awake 18, 155
Backward 77
Ball 95
Banana 110
Bandage 170
Bathtub 83
Beans 110
Bear 182
Beautiful 141
Bed 18
Bedroom 83
Bee 152, 182
Berry 110
Bird 182
Black 126
Block 95
Blood 170
Blue 126
Body 78
Book 35, 95
Boot 128, 152
Bored 60
Boy 75
Brave 60
Break 170
Broccoli 110
Brother 75
Brown 126
Bug 153, 182
Bump 18
Burn 170
Bus 95, 167
Butterfly 153, 182
Cake 110

Calendar 141
Calm 46
Candle 150
Candy 111, 148
Candy Cane 150
Car 167
Carrot 111
Cat 75, 183
Caterpillar 153, 183
Chair 84, 95
Cheese 111
Chicken 111, 183
Choice 96
Circle 96, 131
City 167
Cleanup 43
Clear 141, 155
Close (door) 42
Cloud 141, 155
Coat 43, 96, 128
Cold 141, 155
Come 43
Community 167
Cookie 111
Corn 111, 148
Cow 183
Crayon 96
Cup 112
Dance 78
Danger 170
Dark 126, 148, 155
Day 141
Deaf 28
Dentist 167
Different 156
Doctor 167
Dog 75, 183
Don't Know 42
Don't Like 42, 112
Don't Want 42, 112
Door 84
Dry 156
Ear 78
Eat 112

Egg 112
Elbow 78
Embarrassed 60
Emergency 911 171
Every Day 42
Excited 60
Eye 78
Face 60, 78
Fall 148
Fall (down) 79
Family 75
Farm 183
Farmer 168
Father 75
Favorite 96
Feast 148
Feet 79
Female 76
Ferry Boat 168
Find 96
Finger Spelling 35
Finish 43
Fire/Burn 171
Firefighter 168
Fish 76, 112, 184
Flower 153
Focus 43
Forget 43, 73
Freeze 142, 150
Friday 142
Friend 97
Friendly 44, 60
Frog 153, 184
Full 61
Funny 61
Game 97
Get 44
Gift 150
Girl 76
Glasses 129
Glove 129
Glue 97
Go 44, 97, 184
Grandfather 76

Grandmother 76
Grapes 113
Grass 153
Green 126
Grow 154
Hamburger 113
Hands 79
Happy 61
Have/Has 73
Head 79
Hearing 28
Heart 79
Hello 44
Help 44, 171
Here 184
Hide 79, 184
Home 97
Horse 76, 184
Hot 142, 156
Hot Dog 113
House 84
How Many? 147
Hungry 61, 113
Hurt 61, 171
I/Me 44, 128
Ice 142, 150
Ice Cream 113
Insect 153, 182
Juice 113
Jump 80
Jump Rope 80
Kitchen 84
Kite 154
Knee 80
Kneel 80
Leaf 148
Lettuce 114
Librarian 168
Library 97
Light 126, 156
Like 114
Line Up 45
Lion 185
Listen 45
Live 185
Lock 45, 73
Lonely 61
Look For 98
Lunch 98, 114
Mad 62
Mail Carrier 168
Male 75

Man 17
Mask 149
Mean 62
Meat 114
Milk 114
Minute 142
Monday 142
Monkey 185
Month 142
Moon 149
More 114
Morning 18, 143
Mother 76
Mountain 150
Mouse 185
Mouth 80
Nervous 62
Nice 62
Night 143
No 45
Noise/Noisy 45
Noodle 115
Not 18, 45
Not Safe 171
Not Yet 46
Now 143
Numbers 1–20 147
Ocean 185
Old 17
Once in a While 144
Opposites 156
Orange 115, 127
Outdoors 98, 143
Outside 98, 143
Own(s) 73
Paint 98
Pants 129
Paper 98
Pea 115
Peaceful 46
Peach 115
Peanut Butter 115
Pear 115
Pen 98
Pencil 99
Pets 77
Pick Up 73
Picture 84
Pie 116
Pig 185
Pizza 116
Play 99

Please 46, 116
Police 168
Popcorn 116
Possess(es) 73
Post Office 169
Potato 116
Pouring 17
Proud 62
Pumpkin 149
Purple 127
Put Away 99
Quiet 46
Rabbit 186
Rain 17, 143, 156
Rainbow 154
Read 35, 99
Receive 44
Rectangle 131
Red 127
Refrigerator 84
Remember 46, 73
Rice 116
Ride 80
Right (accurate, correct) 74
Roll 81
Rose 154
Rule 46
Ruler 99
Run 81
Sad 62
Safe 171
Safety 171
Sandwich 117
Saturday 143
Scared 63
School 100
Science 100
Second 142
See 128
Sentence 35
Sheep 186
Shirt 129
Shock 172
Shoes 129
Show 81
Shower 85
Shy 63
Sick 63, 172
Sign 28, 100
Silly 63
Sing 81, 100
Sister 77

Sit 46, 81
Skate 150
Ski 151
Skirt..........................129
Sky 144
Sled 151
Slide..........................100
Slow..........................47
Smoke 172
Snack 117
Snake 186
Snob 63
Snoring..........................18
Snow..........................144, 151
Snowboard 151
Snowman 151
Sofa 85
Sometimes..........................144
Soup 117
Spider..........................149, 186
Spin 81
Spring 154
Square 131
Stand..........................46, 82
Stapler..........................100
Star..........................151
Sting 172
Stomach..........................82
Stop..........................47, 172
Story 35, 101
Student..........................101
Sugar..........................117
Summer..........................157

Sun..........................144, 157
Sunday 144
Surprise 63
Swing..........................101
Table 85, 101
Tea 117
Teacher..........................101, 169
Teeter-totter..........................101
Teeth..........................82
Telephone 102, 172
Teletypewriter..........................28
Thank You 47, 117
Think 130
Thirsty..........................64, 118
Thursday..........................144
Time 47, 102, 145
Tiptoe..........................82
Tired 64
Today 145
Toe 82
Toilet..........................47, 85
Tomorrow 145
Tongue 82
Tortilla..........................118
Tow..........................169
Town..........................167
Trade..........................118
Traffic Light 169
Tree 152
Triangle 131
Truck 169
Tuesday..........................145
Turkey 149, 186

Turtle..........................186
Umbrella..........................154
Veterinarian..........................169
Wait..........................48
Walk..........................83
Watch (verb) 74, 83
Water 118
Watermelon 118
Weather 145
Wednesday 146
Week..........................146
What 130
What's Wrong?..........................173
When 130
Where 130
Which 74
White 127
Who..........................74, 130, 187
Why 130
Wind..........................146
Window 85
Windy 157
Winter 152, 157
Wolf..........................187
Word 35
Write..........................36, 102
Wrong..........................48
Yellow 127
Yes..........................48
Yesterday..........................146
Zoo..........................187

SAMPLE LETTER TO FAMILIES

Dear Families,

This year we will be including American Sign Language in our school program. American Sign Language, or ASL, is a visual language that uses hand movements and facial expressions. It is the third most commonly used language in the United States today, and a common way to communicate for people who are deaf.

Your children will benefit from learning ASL for many reasons.

• Signing is very engaging to young children.

• Signing helps them focus on their school activities.

• Children love to use their bodies and move while they are learning!

• Sign language helps children learn new vocabulary words and understand letters and letter sounds.

• Sign language provides another way to communicate needs, feelings, and ideas for young children who sometimes have speaking difficulties.

• Children will be learning a "foreign" language.

• Learning about sign language and people who are deaf helps children understand and appreciate differences.

We will be teaching American Sign Language vocabulary and phrases through stories, games, poems, and songs. Signing will be included in many of our daily school activities, including reading and writing lessons.

Soon your child will be coming home and sharing her new skills with the rest of the family. Excitement in learning ASL is contagious so in the next few weeks **we will begin sending home packets with the illustrations for the new signs we are learning. This isn't homework—just an opportunity for your children to practice their new signing skills at home.**

We hope you will enjoy this part of our program. If you have any questions about ASL or want to learn more about the benefits of learning to sign for young hearing children, just ask!

Sincerely,

REFERENCES

Cooper, B. (2002, October). The use of sign language to teach reading to kindergartners. *The Reading Teacher, 56*, 116–120. Retrieved April 23, 2003, from Expanded Academic database.

Daniels, M. (2001). *Dancing with words: signing for hearing children's literacy*. Westport, CT: Greenwood Publishing.

Donovan, P. (2000). ECRC begins sign-language program. *University of Buffalo Reporter, 32* (4). Retrieved April 3, 2003, from www.buffalo.edu/reporter/vol32/n4.

Ellison, G., Baker, S., & Baker, P. (1982, May). Hand to hand: the joy of signing among hearing children. *Young Children*, 53–58.

Felzer, L. (1998, Winter). A multi-sensory reading program that really works. *Teaching and Change, 5* (2), 169–183. Retrieved January 22, 2002, from ProQuest database.

Garcia, J. (1999). *Sign with your baby*. Bellingham, WA: Stratton-Kehl Publications.

Goodwyn, S., Acredolo, L., & Brown, C. (2000). Impact of symbolic gesturing on early language development. *Journal of Nonverbal Behavior*, (24), 81–103.

Hafer, J.C., & Wilson, R.M. (1986). *Signing for reading success*. Washington, DC: Gallaudet University Press.

Heller, I., Manning, D., Pavur, D., & Wagner, K. (1998, Jan.–Feb.). Let's all sign: enhancing language development in an inclusive preschool. *Teaching Exceptional Children*, 50–53.

Lohmann, B. (1999, April 7). A time to speak. *Richmond Times Dispatch*, p. D1.

Manning-Beagle, D. (1988). Learning through motion: sign language for young children. In E. Jones (Ed.), *Reading, writing, and talking with four, five, and six year olds*. Pasedena, CA: Pacific Oaks College.

Stokoe, W. (1960). *Sign language structure*. Silver Spring, MD: Linstok Press.

RESOURCES

Dictionaries

Bahan, B., & Dannis, J. (1994). *Signs for me: Basic vocabulary for children, parents, and teachers.* San Diego, CA: DawnSign Press.

Chambers, D. (1998). *Communicating in Sign.* Brooklyn, NY: Amaranth.

Fant, L. (1994). *American Sign Language phrase book.* Chicago, IL: Contemporary Books.

Flodin, M. (1994). *Signing illustrated.* New York: Perigee Books.

Hafer, J.C., & Wilson, R.M. (1996). *Come sign with us.* Washington, DC: Gallaudet University Press.

Humphries, T., & Padden, C. (1994). *A basic course in American Sign Language.* Silver Spring, MD: T.J. Publishers.

Kramer, J. (1999). *You can learn sign language.* Kirkland, WA: Troll Communications.

McKinney, V., & Vega, R. (1997). *The picture plus dictionary.* Hillsboro, OR: Butte Publishing.

Proctor, C. (1995). *Multilingual dictionary of American Sign Language.* Chicago, IL: NTC Publishing.

Riekehof, L. (1987). *The joy of signing.* Springfield, MO: Gospel Publishing House.

Sternberg, M. (1981). *American Sign Language dictionary.* New York: Harper and Row.

Children's Books

Aseltine, L. (1986). *I'm deaf and it's o.k.* Niles, IL: Whitman and Company.

Bahan, B., & Dannis, J. (1994). *My ABC signs of animal friends.* San Diego, CA: DawnSign Press.

Baker, P. (1986). *My first book of sign.* Washington, DC: Gallaudet University Press.

Bove, L. (1985). *Sesame Street sign language ABC.* New York: Random House.

Chaplin, S. (1986). *I can sign my ABC's.* Washington, DC: Gallaudet University Press.

Charlip, R., Miller, M., & Ancona, G. (1987). *Handtalk Birthday.* New York: Four Winds Press.

Flodin, M. (1991). *Signing for kids.* New York: Berkley Publishing Group.

Greenberg, J. (1985). *What's the sign for friend?* New York: Franklin Watts.

Lakin, P. (1994). *Dad and me in the morning.* Morton Grove, IL: Albert Whitman and Company.

Lowell, G. (2000). *Elana's ears.* Washington, DC.: Magination Press.

Millman, I. (2000). *Moses goes to school.* New York: Frances Foster Books.

Millman, I. (2002). *Moses goes to a concert.* Elgin, IL: Sunburst Publishing.

Millman, I. (2003). *Moses goes to the circus.* New York: Frances Foster Books.

Millman, I. (2004). *Moses goes to a play.* New York: Frances Foster Books.

Peterson, J. (1977). *I have a sister, my sister is deaf.* New York: Harper and Row.

Rankin, L. (1998). *The handmade alphabet.* New York: Puffin Press.

Rankin, L. (1998). *The handmade counting book.* New York: Dial Books.

Shroyer, S., & Kimmel, J. (1987). *1 2 3 Sign with me.* Greensboro, NC: Sugar Sign Press.

Videos and Classroom Materials

ASL Fairy Tales I &II. (1986) Paul Chamberlain.

Blue's Clues: All kinds of signs. (2001) VHS Paramount Studio.

Second step conflict resolution program. (2002) Seattle, WA: Committee for Children.

Signing time volumes I & II. (2002).

Sign me a story. (1987) Signed by Linda Bove. Sony Video.

Sound and fury. (2002) DVD by New Video Group, New York.

Visual Tales. Signed by Billy Seago. Sign-a-Vision.

Sign language flash cards, lotto games, vocabulary and song books, and posters available at www.garlicpress.com.

Further Reading

Carney, J., Cioffi, G., & Raymond-White, M. (1985, Spring). Using sign language for teaching sight words. *Teaching Exceptional Children, 17* (3), 214–217.

Good, L., Feekes, J., & Shawd, B. (1993, Winter). Let your fingers do the talking: hands-on language learning through signing. *Childhood Education, 70* (2), 81–84. Retrieved January 12, 2002, from Infotrac database.

Greene, L., & Dicker, E. (1981). *Discovering sign language.* Washington, DC: Gallaudet University Press.

Kokette, S. (2000). Sign language: The best second language? *Indy's Child.* Retrieved January 13, 2002, from www.littlesigners.com/article 12.

Lane, H. (1984). *When the mind hears: A history of the Deaf.* New York: Random House.

Lane, H. (1996). *A journey into the Deaf World.* San Diego, CA: Dawn Sign Press.

Lane, H. (1999). *The mask of benevolence: disabling the Deaf community.* San Diego, CA: Dawn Sign Press.

Lawrence, C. (2002). Using sign language in your classroom. *Paper presented at the Annual Convention for Exceptional Children.* Retrieved April 18, 2003, from ERIC database.

Maher, J. (1996). *Seeing language in Sign.* Washington, DC: Gallaudet University Press.

McNight, J. (1979, November). Using the manual alphabet in teaching reading to learning disabled children. *Journal of Learning Disabilities, 12*, 581–584.

Neisser, A. (1983). *The other side of silence: sign language and the Deaf community in America.* New York: Alfred A. Knopf.

Padden, C., & Humphries, T. (1988). *Deaf in America: voices from a culture.* Cambridge, MA: Harvard University Press.

Sacks, O. (1989). *Seeing voices. A journey into the world of the Deaf.* Berkeley, CA: University of California Press.